# THE WIRED CHURCH 2.0

# THE WIRED CHURCH 2.0

**LEN WILSON**
with JASON MOORE

Abingdon Press
*Nashville*

# THE WIRED CHURCH 2.0

*Copyright © 2008 by Len Wilson*

*This book is printed on acid-free paper.*

**Library of Congress Cataloging-in-Publication Data**

Wilson, Len, 1970-
  The wired church 2.0 / Len Wilson with Jason Moore.
    p. cm.
  ISBN 978-0-687-64899-3 (binding: pbk., adhesive, perfect : alk. paper)
  1. Public worship--Audio-visual aids. 2. Church work--Audio-visual aids. I. Moore, Jason. II. Title. III. Title: Wired church two point zero.

  BV288.W55 2008
  254'.3--dc22

                                                            2008016647

Scripture quotations marked NIV are taken from the Holy Bible, NEW INTERNATIONAL VERSION®. Copyright © 1973, 1978, 1984 by International Bible Society. All rights reserved throughout the world. Used by permission of International Bible Society.

08 09 10 11 12 13 14 15 16 17—10 9 8 7 6 5 4 3 2 1
MANUFACTURED IN THE UNITED STATES OF AMERICA

# CONTENTS

Bonus Materials available at www.thewiredchurch2.com

"We tend to overestimate the effect of a technology in the short run and underestimate the effect in the long run."—Roy Amara

PART ONE

# DEVELOPING A MISSION FOR MEDIA

# CHAPTER 1
# UNDERSTANDING DIGITAL MEDIA

I recently spoke to a group of about thirty-five pastors about "digital ministry." During the question and answer time, I heard the same old argument I often hear made against media: "Let me caution you," a pastor said. "Sometimes it's important to be able to come away from media, and not let it get in the way of the message. Sometimes there just isn't an image that works, so at my church we keep it simple. There are some weeks we don't even use the screen."

Maybe you share the view of this iconoclast.[1] As an advocate for digital media and image in worship, I may go to my grave hearing this same objection from some church professionals. I acknowledged that, yes, some weeks are more difficult than others to image, but when we decide to make it "simple" on ourselves, we are making a decision to make it more difficult on our congregations.

The questioner's argument raised some questions for me, such as: How many church professionals, regardless of denomination, confuse the small "w," the printed words of the Bible, for the big "W," the living Word of Jesus Christ, and in the process sacralize print as a holy form of communication and demonize image as a luxury, or worse, as untrustworthy? How do some preachers who have been trained in the value of homiletics so blindly ignore the value of story and the role of metaphor in rhetoric when

communicated through a visual medium? How many of the same preachers still fail to see that in many parts of the Bible, truth is story and story
is truth, and metaphor is about as biblical as you can get, whether God is
a bush, the Holy Spirit is a dove, or we are clay or sheep or children, and
that message and media are inseparable, messily mixed together? The oral
practice of preaching was profoundly influenced by print and text, and will
again be by screens and image, whether we like it or not. There were many,
many people who once violently fought the introduction of print technology into worship, just as now happens with new media.

# A SIMPLE DEFINITION OF MEDIA

The problem may be rooted in confusion about what exactly media is.
*Media* is the plural form of the word *medium*, which is an agent for transmitting messages between senders and receivers. Messages can be anything
from the verbal "I love you," to a printed direct mail card, to images on
screens, to the civil warning siren that goes off in rural towns twice a
month. Electronic, or digital, media are a means to send a message or set
of messages to individuals or groups of people in which electronic forms of
technology are used. Traditionally the electronic forms have consisted of
a group of mass communication tools such as radio, film, television, and the
Internet ("mass communication" being a term for the means by which
masses of people receive the same sent message).

In popular culture, the term *media* has come to signify any form of mass
communication, and even the industry that creates its messages. Further,
*digital media* refers to this set of communication tools as a singular group-
ing, particularly in reference to the profound cultural changes they have
brought about since the beginning of the twentieth century.

As distinct from detached analysis and criticism, digital, visual media
is characteristically narrative in form, which means that it is adept at
telling stories. This narrative purpose is in direct contrast to mass print
culture, the culture of book reading and research that preceded electronic
media.[2] Its strength in storytelling is due to powerful engagement of the
senses on multiple levels through visual and aural imagery.

The definition of mass, digital media is evolving as its technological
components mature and become more dynamic. Business environments
have global, face-to-face boardroom videoconferences; friends communicate real-time by chat, IM, and Twitter, then meet up at the local café
using each other's GPS coordinates; groups of fans even persuade television

networks to rethink programming decisions through grassroots digital campaigns such as the one that Jason participated in one lazy Sunday when he made a homemade YouTube video and helped save the cult favorite show *Jericho*. The rise of democratic, participatory media—often called Web 2.0—is signaling a maturation of this new digital communications macrosystem. In many ways it parallels the rise of the printing press from an agent of maintenance to an agent of change over 500 years ago. What it means for the church is that we now have the ability as Martin Luther once did to harness this new media to communicate the gospel in ways that we might not even imagine.

To fully respond to the pastor's statement, it's not a question of whether or not we should "come away from media, and not let it get in the way of the message." The question is, which media—which forms of communication—do we believe are worthy of communicating the gospel? Whether subconscious or not, the questioning pastor revealed that he preferred the more established medium of mass print in worship. The underlying philosophical proposition of this book is that image is just as worthy and capable, and in some ways, a more powerful and effective way to communicate the gospel in this time. (Ironically, there was once a time in church history when the printed word was new and mistrusted, and images were established and "traditional.")

Media is not simply an add-on to the existing means of communicating the gospel in worship, but an emerging, fundamentally new system of communication, equal to the oral and written word. It is imperative that today's Christian leaders understand and use media effectively in worship.

Media, then, should not be treated as operational support, but as a ministry that uses video, audio, graphics, text, the Internet, and other emerging technology applications to communicate the gospel. The more digital, narrative, participatory, and immersive, the better.

# MEDIA AS A GOSPEL-SHARING MISSION

At a workshop on media in congregational ministry, a listener questioned me about the specific costs involved in producing high-quality media. He was concerned that it was simply too expensive to do on a weekly basis. I outlined a cost comparison between funding media ministry and funding more established communication forms, such as newsletters and organs. When I mentioned the organ, a man in the back of the room groaned and interrupted with the exclamation that his church had spent $1.3 million for a new organ. He was mortified because he realized that his church had spent so much money ensuring continued success at speaking to a small faction of his church culture through an organ. Now, his church is impoverished when it comes time to speak to much of his congregation, and the culture outside of the church walls, through digital media.

Regardless of its resources, a church is likely to fail without a clear purpose for what a media ministry should accomplish. There are unfortunately many tragic tales of churches that have bought a van full of equipment, only to realize their outsized efforts have produced little effective ministry. An effective mission statement is crucial for the beginning of a viable media ministry. Ideas drive technology, not the other way around.

Media ministry is demanding. Once a congregation realizes it has digital communications opportunities via video, graphic images, and the Internet at its disposal, seemingly every ministry in the church will want to utilize them for its own needs. While each ministry in the life of a church is important, a fledgling media ministry won't be able to meet every demand. A written mission statement keeps members focused on what is important. Having a clear purpose enables both the media minister or church leader and the congregation or staff to keep clear-eyed and objective about what is possible before powering up the tools.

A mission statement will lead to judicious spending of limited funds, support of key programs, and an understanding of what digital media look like and are intended to do.

When I started on full time in "electronic media" at Ginghamsburg United Methodist Church in 1995, my first order was to get the projector in focus. At the time, the task literally took a day. Having done that, I needed to figure out how to translate the theories of my education into the life of a congregation. So my second "to do" item was to create a mission statement. It had three parts:

1. Make excellent media.
2. Make media ministry integral to the life of the church.
3. Encourage a level of media literacy so that eventually each area of ministry in the church will create its own digital media, just as they currently make their own brochures and other written documents.

Underneath these three points of purpose was the firm belief that (what was still called) electronic media was equally important as spoken and written communication in its ability to communicate the gospel, and maybe even more important in the media-driven culture in which we live.

This was my mission for media. Use the following chapters to help you create your own unique mission for spreading the gospel in today's digital language.

# CHAPTER 2

# FOUR WAYS TO UNDERSTAND MEDIA IN MINISTRY

Media ministry is broad and may take on many different forms. This book will help you understand some of these distinctions and their impact on ministry decisions.

Universities construct fields of discipline in a helpful way. At a large university a student has the option to pursue media through fine arts (a theater or literature major, for example); through traditional, mass forms such as radio and television (mass communication major); through oral communication (speech major); through tactile forms (art majors); through written forms (English or journalism majors); or through computer technology (information systems major). Each is a valid media form. Each addresses specific media as communication tools. Some of the ways, then, to understand the potential role of media may be characterized into the following four categories.

## 1. MEDIA AS THE ARTS

One understanding of media is defined as a means to (re)create the impact and experience of fine art. The fine arts have been traditionally thought of as stage, dance, sculpture, literature, painting, poetry, (what is now known as) classical music, film, and so on. Prior to the twentieth century the purpose of the arts for the church was to re-create the divine through representations of beauty and truth. The theological basis for the arts is largely one that views God as the manifestation of all that is good, beautiful, and true. Applied to the gospel, the arts aim to create a response in which the receiver perceives God through interpretations that engage the soul and the spirit.

To create a broad typology, art may be classified one of three ways: fine, folk, and pop.

Prior to the electronic age, fine arts set the cultural standard. After its inception as a state religion under Constantine in the fourth century, Christianity became the keeper of fine art and through it the standard-bearer for cultural norms. Pope Gregory made the announcement at the dawn of the seventh century that the arts were the primary means to disciple the uneducated. He called the arts "the Bible for the illiterate." The cultural Renaissance of the fifteenth and sixteenth centuries was fueled by the arts, and was to a degree subsidized by the church, particularly in the areas of music and sculpture. Persons of all socioeconomic backgrounds partook of the arts.

Beginning in the late-nineteenth century, however, there was a transition in Western culture away from the fine arts as the cultural pacesetter. This coincided with a detachment in the relationship of art and the church. The fine arts have become increasingly abstract, ambiguous, and driven by an abandonment of the notion of objective truth. The worldview of fine artists has become increasingly relativistic, losing the Judeo-Christian value system of its religious and cultural benefactors.

Disconnected from the contemporary fine art scene, many in the church turn to historical art, particularly from the Renaissance era, as a means to visually communicate the gospel.

Others in the church have embraced the rise of what may be referred to as "folk art," or art created by and for specific social groups (often beyond our own experience). Folk art is created by self-taught artists and reflects indigenous social experience, and is mostly independent of the trends and movements of fine art.

As electronic and then digital media have permeated society, a third type of art has risen that captures more common creative expressions. This type of art, often called commercial or pop art, has become dominant. *Time* magazine, in a commemorative issue on the top artists and entertainers of the twentieth century, said, "Literature, the theater, classical music [have] lost the authority to set the cultural agenda. Today, the influence, the action, the buzz is all pop."[1] Pop art has replaced fine art.

Some art advocates in the church speak of the need to "reclaim" the arts for the kingdom of God. This desire is commendable if art is once again an agent of the gospel, sponsored by and created with the aid of the church. What will not happen, however, at least in our lifetime, is a return of the fine arts to a former position of cultural authority, granted by sacred benefactors.

This shift is not to be mourned. The rules have simply changed. Pop art isn't the absence of art, as some fine art connoisseurs proclaim; its artistic beauty is in part found in its commonality. Creative expression in the digital age has become democratic. God would have it that way. According to Genesis, God created all people in the image of the Creator. All people, thus, are creative. And with the birth of the new communication system of digital media, many more people have the opportunity to express their innate creativity. And the consequences of that opportunity are proving explosive even within the communication arts. People with no formal media training post homemade videos to YouTube, blogs, or Facebook pages. A fourteen-year-old in media ministry gave me the URL for her website. Software enables children to create 3-D computer animation. Many of the savviest members of local church media ministries are teenagers or even tween-agers. The opportunities are incredible, and they do not require the same degree of training as the fine arts demanded and regulated for entry into an academy or guild.

The narrative theologian Frederick Buechner says that the most powerful preaching for this age comes from the poets, playwrights, and novelists. He almost got it right, with amends for his print-age bias. The most powerful preaching today is actually coming from the filmmakers, the stand-up comedians, and the producers—the storytellers of the digital age.

Media is most effective as a communication system when it expresses art for the cultural majority. There are always subcultures present, which are to be addressed. But the primary, the global reach of media is reflected through pop art expression. A return to fine arts is a "retro" move.

Our job, as messengers of the gospel, is to speak in whatever language the culture is speaking. If Renaissance history is any barometer, we are about to ride a wave of explosive creativity, as this new medium grows out of prepubescent awkwardness and becomes fully assimilated into the lives of those with truth to speak, with media that forces the receivers out of their state of indifference.[2]

# 2. MEDIA AS INFORMATION

Manifestations of electronic media through the twentieth century have been primarily documentation, rather than interpretation. Radio, television, and now the Internet, the three largest mass mediums, have been known more for the ability to disseminate information globally than for the ability to represent artistic truth. Most early radio professionals came from print culture disciplines such as the newspaper business; likewise, the heritage of television is radio. All three disciplines feed the Internet. Television was touted as the first global medium, and its biggest victories came not through M*A*S*H and *Dallas*, both internationally popular programs, but in its ability to alert the world to breaking news stories as they happened. Vietnam was the first living room war. The world watched the British monarchy, in all of its pomp, get married. A new synthesis is emerging for the niches of each medium, with daily Internet information (of sometimes questionable repute) existing beside the twenty-four-hour news cycle of talk radio and television, which is so valuable in times of crisis such as 9/11 and so annoying when there is no actual story to cover.

Mass media, as distinct from the artistic understanding of media, have traditionally been used primarily as means of information, a way to reach masses of people quickly. Many early attempts by the church to use electronic media, mimicking the culture, approached it in this fashion. Mainline denominations constructed entire global news and information agencies for the purpose of processing and disseminating information. The thinking was, rather than report bad news or conflict, the church would report good news, and people's lives would be transformed.

But we have learned again that transmitting information is not the same thing as empowering transformation. The late twentieth century's move away from the notion of objective truth destroys the ministry promise of media as information. Postmodern culture responds, "My truth is not the same as your truth, so who cares?"

The use of media as an informational tool has been incomplete in transforming people into Christ's likeness. Readers may cognitively see or hear the power of Christ's love but not be moved to act upon it themselves because it doesn't engage their soul and spirit as art does. Media as information, then, is the opposite of media as art. But neither is complete. As Jesus said, love the Lord your God with all of your heart, mind, and soul (see Matthew 22:37). The commandment is to use all three faculties, not one or another. Information isn't enough; presentation matters. Effective or excellent media for this age engages not only the mind but also the heart and soul.

# 3. MEDIA AS MISSION OR EVANGELISM

The third use of media is for evangelism, for the purpose of drawing unchurched people into a faith community. This view recognizes that media is the central communication component of Western and increasingly global social life, and it sees media as a primary means in which to speak the culture's language. However, media in this use is for speaking outside the walls of the church community, and is not for the most part a central communication form within church life. Worship practices and discipleship forms within church life remain steeped in pre-digital culture. Media is only used for outreach or evangelism purposes, such as the occasional advertising campaign, out of a vague awareness that it is important at high times in the Christian year to do a little promotion.

One problem with speaking the cultural language to the world but not to the church is that the product cannot match the advertisement. Any person will try something once. If the reality does not match the hype, then that person, the visitor, won't try again. An effective way to turn people away is to pull a "bait-and-switch" by promoting one thing, only to actually present another, that is, to imply media-savvy in communicating spiritual truth but to provide hymnals and attempts at fine art (that often aren't so fine) upon arrival. The effect is similar to the promotional material that comes in the mail announcing a free cruise, but which can only be obtained, according to fine print restrictions, by purchasing a condominium. Advocates holler with zeal, "Truth in advertising!"

It's not even that the messages aren't truthful. It's that the culture is media-savvy. It does little good to draw in visitors at a surface level when there is no system in place to continue speaking their language once they arrive.

Contemporary effective messages must speak on multiple levels, using vertical communication and not only horizontal communication. Simply put, the church should not advertise in the marketplace (horizontally) until it is capable of delivering messages that are integrated with its internal communication matrix (vertically). For example, with the Internet, many corporations have learned that they cannot handle an effective presence on the Web without structurally supporting that through a pervasive

Intranet, or an internal computer networking base. Similarly, churches should be careful to create continuity between their external and internal communication and media use.

Another problem with the evangelistic approach to media is that increasingly even those within the walls of the church are media-savvy. Churches fighting "contemporary" and "traditional" worship wars often don't realize that the issue may be framed as communication. Churchgoers are also cultural participants, and they are adept at both understanding digital media's messages and deconstructing the medium that delivers them.

To be in ministry means maintaining the constant tension between life in the Holy Spirit and life on Earth. It means seeing the secular culture as incorrect, but not evil, and the job of the church to transform the outer culture to its rightful place as the kingdom of God. Salvation is not just for another time and place but for all people, now. Living in the gap of where we are in Christ and where the culture is without Christ, tense though that place may be, is where Christians are called to serve, because it is the only place in which the world can hear our messages. It does not mean living a dualistic life in which church culture is separate from secular culture. If in the risen Christ, the Holy Spirit abides with us, and God is not confined to the physical location of the Temple, then that means there shouldn't be sacred and secular divisions. Our whole lives, including the means by which we communicate, become integrated. We use the same media, or means of communicating, on Sunday morning as we do on Saturday night. And with the presence of the Holy Spirit, all become sanctified.

# 4. MEDIA AS CULTURAL LANGUAGE

The combination of the best of these three understandings of media, then, forms a fourth: media as cultural language. It should (a) learn from innovation in pop cultural artistic expression, (b) reach the heart, mind, and soul, (c) through its expression of Christ and truth, draw people to God, and (d) mediate the presence of the church in the world, for the sake of transforming the culture.

Cable television and satellite television, sending improved digital signals to our high-definition televisions on hundreds of channels, still haven't solved the basic issue that "nothing's on." A lack of content has never been an issue for the gospel storyteller. The challenge of the church is the opposite of the cultural challenge. Hollywood struggles for good stories to tell. Our task is to take our powerful, life-changing story and present it in such a way that people understand.

Ezra did just that. After a long, dark night, things were coming to-gether for the Israelites. Jerusalem's walls had been rebuilt, and the Tem-ple was next. Ezra, who had been commissioned with the proclamation of the Law, finally got the opportunity to read it before the Israelites. Except he had a problem. The cultural language from the making of the Law to the present day had changed, possibly to Aramaic, the language of the Is-raelites' Babylonian and Persian captors. So Ezra had Levite priests be an interpretive public address system, standing among the people as he read the Law. Nehemiah 8:8 (NIV) says, "They read from the Book of the Law of God, making it clear [translating it] and giving the meaning so that the people could understand what was being read." The consequence? Verse 9 says they wept for joy at the hearing of the Law, the Word of their God, be-cause they finally understood. It had been spoken in their language.

The gospel is powerful and attractive: any effective presentation of the Word of God has the potential to result in a life-changing experience for those who receive it. For the media age, the challenge of ministers of any capacity is to speak with the same lucidity using our cultural language of media that the Levite priests did when they translated the Law for the peo-ple. If done well, the result will be changed lives and a renewed church.

# CHAPTER 3

# THE SHAPE OF THIS CULTURAL LANGUAGE

## STORYTELLING

The messages that digital media send may be classified as story, which is a colloquialism but also a reference to what Leonard Sweet calls the "ancient future," or a postmodern reinterpretation of the oral culture of early civilizations, in which the primary communication tool was the story.

Noted media theorist George Gerbner defines storytelling as the "shorthand" for the "magic" that is created out of our unique ability as a species to live in a world larger than our own immediate gratifications. It is the compilation of these stories that composes the seamless web of our culture.[1] In this understanding, stories are not fiction but reflections of the deeper reality that frame the messages we send to one another, individually and collectively, to edify and serve one another and the world around us.

In the mass print age, storytelling took a backseat to more formal symbiotic relationships. But the twenty-first century has seen a resurgence of the metaphor as communication tool.

The concept of storytelling is apropos for digital media, as its components lend themselves to narrative forms. Stories engage multiple senses.

Visual and aural imagery add multiple dimensions of depth to the process of telling a story.

One framework for developing media, and beyond media for developing worship, that engages this culture is to evaluate the presence of story. How much story is in your work? There are three types of story to find. One is cultural story. These are the broad, shared experiences of our lives. They can be factual events such as 9/11, trends such as the rise of personal, mobile media, or the "tentpole" film stories of common experience that keep film studios afloat every summer and Christmas season.

Another type of story is biblical story. Worship design that loses the "scripture reading" portion of liturgy does a grave disservice to believers by reducing the presence of biblical story to prooftexts supporting talking points on doctrine or Christian life. There is great power in the entirety of biblical story, especially when it is presented through nontextual means, such as orally or by visual, digital technology.

A third type of story arises out of our communal experiences as believers in a body of Christ. Traditionally, this took the form of a testimony in worship. For the digital age, it is engaging and effective to hear a two-minute personal faith story through the medium of video, with an edited first-person retelling over an appropriate soundtrack and shots of the teller's environment interspersed throughout. This is much more compelling than the twenty minutes it would take the same person to awkwardly tell the story, using nothing but a microphone and a podium.

Jesus, a storyteller, would have been a natural communicator for the digital media age: he used intimate distance, involving small groups with stories, parables, and images. Although fluent in the Law and possibly in three languages (Hebrew, Greek, and Aramaic) by the age of twelve, Jesus did not communicate in the methodology of the Temple thinkers, but instead he chose to speak to the populace in a language that they could understand. Obviously, his message was heard. It is the reception of the story that is critical.

# EXCELLENCE

Remember *Wayne's World*? The comedic *Saturday Night Live* sketches and 1992 movie based on them showed two geeks running their own live public access television show from their parents' basement. No one would accuse Wayne and Garth of producing high-quality media. Established by Congress and intended to provide cultural dialogue in an age of broadcast hegemony, public access instead became the forum of video geeks everywhere, and their messages have indeed been varied, but almost always unclear and poorly produced. Blogs, vlogs, YouTube, and other forms of digital distribution have since largely replaced it.

The sudden ubiquity of self-made media has only fanned the flames of mediocrity when it comes to the production values of the church. The online church media market has become flooded with what are often poorly made video clips for worship. The church has been unwilling to make the sacrifices necessary to speak the language of the culture fluently, or with excellence. Our halfhearted messages come out under our breath, slurred and monotone.

I have met a number of producers in Hollywood who have given up on the idea of integrating their faith into their passion for digital media. One was a man who was the associate producer of a long-running daytime game show. He and a number of other professionals with active faith lives had all chosen to live and work in Southern California in the attempt to have positive influence on the culture at large from within the secular entertainment industry. This leader understood the value of excellence, and during our conversation he specifically pointed out attempts at translating the gospel into the cultural language, such as the (in)famous film *The Judas Project*, as a reason he was no longer attempting to integrate his faith and vocation. To him, *The Judas Project* was a poorly done work that did not interpret the gospel in an attractive, visual way. High-quality presentation mattered so much to him that he would rather produce a game show with money prizes, and with a budget, than the gospel story without a budget.

To me, he seemed right about the importance of excellence, but it was frustrating that he had no concept or model of how to tell the gospel story effectively outside of the entertainment business. His quandary reflects a general approach to media ministry within the Christian community, which merely adds a Judeo-Christian veneer to the porous moral mire found in the messages of the entertainment industry.

Our calling is to transform the culture.[2] The world will always be as a whole lost without the transforming power of Jesus Christ. Trying to change the entire culture by a return to the pseudo-Christian days of Ozzie and Harriet will only be met with frustration and failure. The way to transform the culture is through individuals and the work of the congregation. To use a phrase coined by the late Tip O'Neill when he was Speaker of the House, "Think Global, Act Local." True, lasting change occurs one small step at a time. For us this means telling digital media stories in local church contexts for the purpose of evangelism, edification, discipleship, and transformation.

Lack of excellence takes two forms in many congregational media ministries. One is ignorance of the craft, which often comes with a strange pride. We agree on the need to make music professional, but we often dismiss and even fear professionalism in media. The other is media as "Holy Blob of Color," which is a term we use to describe eye candy that says nothing in particular. Excellence requires us to tell these stories with lucidity. The opposite of clear communication is *noise*, another apropos term used in the digital media industry. From a technical standpoint, noise is anything that interferes with a desired signal, whether video or audio. Culturally there is a lot of noise as well. Many recent Hollywood films, particularly during the summer seasons, avoid lucid storytelling, opting for an emphasis on special effects instead of plot development.

In spite of the postmodern emphasis on deconstruction of form, clear communication occurs through a mostly invisible medium. Like the offensive linemen on a football team, a medium that does its job will elicit a score with the receiver, not a focus on its job of blocking out noise. The viewer should not say "What an effect!" but "What a story!" because the focus of the gospel storyteller is to use media technology as tool, not toy.

The democracy of video has created a number of untrained producers who mixed their video effects like so many poor verb tenses. Grungy wipes and textures cannot compensate for a lack of compelling narrative. There is a distinct difference between excellence and entertainment. Be careful with your use of effects when learning to speak the digital media language. Nothing attracts more than a good story. Effects properly used will enhance the telling of the story, not detract.

# INTEGRATION

The pervasiveness of the media age changes the way we conceptualize the use of media. Having a big screen doesn't mean lowering it for a video clip or a graph of the church financial state, then raising it and returning to the good old days of doing church. This is the media equivalent of rolling out the grand piano for a featured music number, then rolling it offstage once it's over. It means integrating imagery, video, and sound into the entire church experience, whether that is worship, education, administration, or outreach. "Raising the screen," or putting media in a compartment, means that the church is not acknowledging its continued dependence on outdated forms of communication.

Many well-meaning inquirers say, "I want to do this to reach the youth." Youth groups are definitely one reason for the incorporation of digital media, because youth and children speak this language innately. As I noted in my acknowledgments to *Digital Storytellers* (Abingdon Press, 2002), my eldest daughter Kaylyn, who was incidentally born on the binary-like date of 11-10-01, will have digital DNA beyond my imagining. Children of the digital age are being raised from birth with its presence surrounding them. They are completely media literate, understanding both how to send messages and how to receive them.

Don't merely use media as a gimmick to reach the youth. Your attempts will be completely transparent and high on their "cheese-ometer."

A media ministry is not only for youth or children. The members and visitors of your congregation, no matter what their age, watch thirty hours of TV per week or more. Older persons are almost as likely to use e-mail as youth. Digital media is saturated throughout the culture. Television became a national phenomenon in the early 1950s, which means that the majority of kids born in the 1940s grew up with a screen. These "youth" are now seventy or older and have seen visual media their entire lives. Digital media is everywhere and for people of all ages. So, as you implement and design media for church life, don't just cater to the "unchurched," or to certain age groups or demographic niches. Make sure media is available to all, inside and out.

Similarly, it is a mistake to assume that the use of digital media in ministry is primarily a form of outreach or mission to the "unchurched." This line of thinking assumes that members of your congregation are separated from the world. As stated earlier, churchgoers are cultural participants as well, to varying degrees at this point and at various points throughout the stages of life. Communicating visually is about connecting with everyone regardless of where they are on the continuum of faith.

However, it is possible and even encouraged to alter the design and layout of media to fit certain demographic groups. Follow the model established by broadcast entities. Lifetime network, aimed at women and an older audience, creates softer looks with its video and animation. Colors are usually light pastels, fonts are script or serif. ESPN, aimed at the adult male, creates bolder looks: lots of vibrant color schemes, with lots of texture and movement. Youth culture media has an edginess and seemingly broken-down construction. Text cannot sit still, but rather shifts about in place; colors are dark and light, connoting a flashiness and disruptive experience; the edges of the frame itself sometimes become visible, drawing attention in a deconstructed way to the very existence of the visual medium sending the messages. This latter style is the closest embodiment to Marshall McLuhan's adage that "the medium is the message," in that the message is expressed as much in the medium and style chosen as in the content itself.

Integration means getting to the point in creative presentation where the screen fully reflects and complements messages being communicated through other, more established media such as the spoken and written word. The screen isn't a white elephant; media ministry means utilizing the screen as part of the overall matrix of church life. Integrated media means creating a blend of communication forms. Every new media system has shifted from a period of ignorance and antagonism toward previous forms to a new, holistic understanding of how they fit together. Socrates and Plato distrusted writing, saying it would produce forgetfulness.[3] In one decree, Pope Leo called printing a gift from God, and at the same time censored it.[4] Early film imitated theater, locking down the camera in the best seat of the house and staying wide all the time to capture the entire stage. The first revolutionary director was D. W. Griffith, who in 1908 introduced two incredible techniques: a close-up of the protagonist and editing between two scenes.[5]

A congregation interested in ministry today doesn't ignore digital media, acting like an ostrich with its head in the sand. Neither does it abandon the traditions of the church. Instead, it reinterprets how the best of tradition combines with innovation to speak to its constituents where they are today. The following three imperatives are crucial to doing this reinterpretation in a God-honoring way.

## 1. Recognize the Dynamic Context of Digital Culture

Even as a "church junkie," theologian Tom Boomershine never stops to listen to televised sermons. He concludes that "the sermon flunks the electronic culture viability test."[6] However, the failure of the sermon to be a viable form in digital culture is just as much the fault of the church's legacy of sermon preparation as it is due to the nature of the medium. Oral presenters are all over our plasma screens, with Comedy Central a prime source. The sermon is not dead. It has merely mutated.

Digital culture is dynamic, and the new reality synthesizes the best of our traditions. A hot trend in creativity and the arts in the first decade of the twenty-first century has been the "mashup," or the creation of new works of art by sampling previous works of art. Before artists had the ability to access archives of material, they referenced one another's work by memory. Now, a digital copy is much more precise. As William Gibson points out:

> Our culture no longer bothers to use words like *appropriation* or *borrowing* to describe those very activities. Today's audience isn't listening at all—it's participating. Indeed, *audience* is as antique a term as *record*, the one archaically passive, the other archaically physical. The record, not the remix, is the anomaly today. The remix is the very nature of the digital. Today, an endless, recombinant, and fundamentally social process generates countless hours of creative product (another antique term?). To say that this poses a threat to the record industry is simply comic. The record industry, though it may not know it yet, has gone the way of the record. Instead, the recombinant (the bootleg, the remix, the mash-up) has become the characteristic pivot at the turn of our two centuries.[7] (italics original)

## 2. Let This Mutation Alter the Way in Which We Communicate

If you preach a sermon over the airwaves or across broadcast television, you shove a round mouth into a square hole. It assumes that the best of one form of communication will work in another, completely different form. Preachers, like the dots on a screen, are "channels" of the same good news. But to put one form into another gives results much like the camera lens that sees a video monitor displaying an image of itself: it loops into nothingness. To change the channel of preaching means that you shed the tactics of the vaudeville showperson and the tactics of the solitary iconoclast to discover how multiple forms of visual and aural communication will help tell the gospel story. Cultural literacy does not mean abandoning other forms of communication. Neil Postman, an electronic media naysayer, is correct when he asserts, "Not everything is televisable."[8] For example, reading a book. Or using the screen in worship as a giant piece of paper. Digital media does not abandon previous mediums. Communicators now have an unprecedented plethora of storytelling options at their disposal.

Every new communication system must be taught. It's a form of literacy. A new language is easiest to learn and retain when one is studying it in the majority culture. Digital media is now that language. It is indigenous, a fundamental cognitive system of communication. Most people have heard the "tongue" since the day they were born. A media-literate person is no longer aware of media as a language or means of communication. In fact, resistance to media ministry usually arises out of ignorance of media as a formational system.

When I finished my formal education I joined many unemployed and underemployed college graduates with degrees in communication and media, probably because media was still institutionally a skill. Most universities taught it only as a means of understanding sociological impact. "True" instruction still occurred at the literate level. But as the print culture fades, its purveyors are discovering what everyone else already knew: media is no longer a profession; it is an entire system of communication. Digital forms coexist at the developmental stage with printed forms of literacy. Now a four-year-old child can edit a video. This means the use of digital media is not a fad or trend. This isn't going away in our lifetime.

## 3. Look to the Best Communicators of the Day for "Style" Tips

The fluent church leader is not just a producer of worship but also a producer of culture by observing and editing the trends of the culture at large. In fact, it is these very trends that often give inspiration that may be adapted to ministry contexts.

However, even while looking to the culture for nuances of this visual, digital language, do not

- Let the meaning within the messages of cultural media determine the meaning within your messages; or
- Become bound only to the forms that inspire you.

Artists set the cultural agenda as much as they imitate it. Most great artists may be classified as either innovators or perfecters. Handel the innovator, Mozart the perfecter. Miles Davis the innovator, Wynton Marsalis the perfecter. As the filmmaker Steven Spielberg once said in an interview:

> We define our times as we live them. Every time a studio plays it safe and says this isn't the right time for a western, some western comes out and succeeds. Who would have thought a costume drama, a love story aboard a boat that sinks, was going to move anybody? The times define them-

selves as we move through time. The pundits that start to predict what's right and wrong, what's good timing or bad timing, I used to listen to that, and recently I just don't. I just sort of shoot in the dark.[9]

A media-literate producer is capable of speaking the language with fluency. Ultimately, Wired Churches don't just use film clips and imagery that mimic trendy cultural styles, but figure out, each in their own way, how to say something new with digital media. A gospel storyteller who can achieve this will empower a human being beyond any message that the world may have to offer.

Some of the best communicators are comedians and mashup artists. These people combine oral discourse with imagery and sound, and sample cultural knowledge to communicate new ideas. (Have you ever seen the online mashup video of the horror film *The Shining* as a touching father-son love story? I'd provide the link to it here for you but the link would surely be changed by the time you read this.) The valedictorians of comedy are still the hosts of late-night television, such as Conan O'Brien. It is no coincidence that Conan restrains his opening monologues to a few minutes, then quickly utilizes other, more creative media forms to keep the channel surfers at bay. There is much to learn by watching television critically.

As we'll see in the next chapter, many people confuse relevance for "entertainment" (a term that, while generally a good thing when it comes to popular culture, is almost always used pejoratively when it comes to the church). The fact of the matter, however, is that media ministry done without care for the stylistic and technological standards of the culture in which we are ministering is neither entertaining nor relevant.

CHAPTER 4

# THE "ENTERTAINMENT" QUESTION

Critics of digital media in worship claim that these forms water down the power of the gospel by turning it into consumer entertainment.[1] Here are four reasons this is not true.

## 1. MEDIA MINISTRY IS NOT VAUDEVILLE

The first attempts at producing electronic media as ministry were practiced by the televangelists, who owe their legacy to characters such as Billy Sunday and Aimee Semple McPherson. These pioneers imitated vaudeville actors, who saw the nickelodeon and the radio as new ways in which to spread their message. Their entrepreneurial spirit laid the framework for the debate about "theology as entertainment," which has festered among Christian circles throughout the twentieth century. Denominations at the time insisted that radio networks provide airtime free of charge for the purpose of spreading the gospel, as a public service. Networks complied, but of course it wasn't long before free time was allocated to Sunday morning, when the cost was cheap for the networks. From the standpoint of mission to those outside the walls of the church, this is the least intelligent time for churches to speak the cultural language. Reaching into the culture, like Paul at the Areopagus, means moving out of the familiar religious times and places and taking the gospel to the culture where it lives, or in the case of television, where the ratings are.

In spite of the opportunity to speak to a culture in its newly formed and fresh language, most established churches again managed to use communication systems as support structures for the status quo. It is analogous to the Roman church's first use of the printing press, to enforce the "correct" Mass to outpost parishes who had adapted the Latin text to fit their milieu. Twentieth-century media entrepreneurs assumed no such preferential treatment from a state or from a culture that was defined by its separation from the church. Though Nielsen hadn't invented his rating system yet, their paid airtime was often in what we now call prime time, meaning that their messages were heard by larger masses of people.

As so often happens in the church, however, medium and message became confused over time, and later mass-media evangelists continued for the most part to model themselves after the vaudeville legacy of their predecessors. (This phenomenon isn't confined to televangelism; when a church insists on the holiness of a particular liturgy or instrument, also known as Christian "sacred cows," they engage in confusion between Jesus and "the horse he rode in on.") A legacy is not without merit; all good preachers model themselves after individuals who are successful at the art of public discourse. However, the methodology and mission for many televangelists are now passé. The challenge, then, is for presenters of new media to reinvent what it means to speak the language of this culture.

# 2. LEGITIMACY QUESTIONS ARE IRRELEVANT TO MOST

We have had three generations of television as the dominant communication form of the culture.[2] As pointed out earlier, highschoolers have grandparents who watched *The Honeymooners* as newlyweds. To deny media as a feasible communication form now would put us among the separatist traditions that are well documented in religious history, from the Essenes to the Amish.

The famous first church debate found in Acts centers around the then hot-button issue of Gentiles, the Law, and life in Christ. Should certain laws be obeyed, or are non-Israelites exempt from the rituals that had characterized God-followers for more than a millennium? As the church became a Gentile-dominant church, the question became moot. At some point, the "entertainment" question will also become moot, so long as the integrity of the gospel is not lost in the translation. Fortunately, media is best when created in teams, which in spiritual terms act as accountability groups.

# 3. THE DISTINCTIONS BETWEEN MEDIA AND ITS MESSAGES

The theological error of the early televangelists tends to overshadow their efforts, however crude, at translating the gospel into a new, mass media. Their eagerness to expose so many people to the good news at once outweighed concern they had about the impact of the media on the message. There has been much debate over media pop guru Marshall McLuhan's idiom, "The medium is the message." Is the media the message? For McLuhan's time, in the 1960s, it was. Media was big news in the decade in which television played a major part in redefining the value system of a society.

The printing press was big news, too, when it came out. It spread as fast as the most impressive digital invention of our time. By 1500, over 20 million books had been printed. And yet, the press was still not a full part of the cultural consciousness. Luther expressed genuine surprise in 1518 that his theses had gotten so widespread.[3]

Eventually, the press was assimilated into daily life. So, now, too, digital media is becoming assimilated into daily life. The same could be said for any innovative communication in church history, from the use of stained glass to a bar instrument called the organ. As engineer and futurist Roy Amara has noted, "We tend to overestimate the effect of a technology in the short run and underestimate the effect in the long run."

When electronic media was new, the dominant model was the entertainment industry, which to generate capital created commercial advertisements to support its programming. (There's debate on whether the focus of the entertainment industry is actually the former instead of the latter.) When television was the dominant model for visual media, it was easy to see all visual media as entertainment.

As media enters a stage of adolescence, we are beginning to see the medium spread to other areas of society. CNN uses YouTube to conduct presidential debates. Video, graphics, and the Internet have become standard teaching techniques in schools and universities. At a more basic level, our thought processes as a society are becoming different; we are no longer bound by the linear nature of the scientific method. "Meaning through experience" may be the best slogan for defining postmodernism. When a congregation is speaking this cultural language it is not entertaining. It is simply communicating the message of the gospel in a way that concurs with how we now think as products of our culture.

# 4. COMMUNICATION ISSUES ARE BIBLICAL AND HISTORICAL TO CHURCH MINISTRY

Those fearful of change may find that the move is less about breaking tradition and more about finding new ways to communicate it. This is exactly what Jesus addresses in his parable of new wine and old wineskins in Matthew 9:16-17. Old skins, filled with new wine, will burst. The wine, or the message, needs to be presented in a new package, a new communication form that won't break down before it gets to the eyes and ears of those who hear it.

The use of digital media in worship is vital to our dominant digital culture because it fits with how the gospel always has been communicated. Jesus' use of story and parable in the first century fits with popular culture's use of digital media to communicate in story and metaphor today. Paul's ability to engage his culture and use its latest media, from writing to roads, fits with our digital technology's present ubiquity. Pope Gregory's blessing on stained glass as the "Bible for the illiterate" fits with the projection screen's facility to bring postliterate people to an experience of the Word. The explosion of innovation and change that occurred in the church during the Reformation, concurrent with the rise of the printing press, parallels the explosion in cultural change occurring today. Even the early growth of The United Methodist Church, as one example from a specific denomination's heritage, is rooted in the innovative use of newspapers and circuit riders to spread the gospel. In each case, adoption of innovative communications technology was met with initial resistance, then gradual acceptance. Sometimes, initial resistance was even violent. As Walter Bagehot stated in 1872, "One of the greatest pains to human nature is the pain of a new idea. It . . . makes you think that after all, your favorite notions may be wrong, your firmest beliefs ill-founded. . . . Naturally, therefore, common men hate a new idea, and are disposed more or less to ill-treat the original man who brings it."[4]

# DEALING WITH NAYSAYERS

Criticism is inevitable. There will always be people who find reasons to oppose whatever new thing is happening in the church, but you can rise above that by focusing on the higher objective. Be willing to take risks. Be willing to try new things, and learn from trends in popular periodicals and television. Be tenacious in the face of miscues and naysayers. Some people will never get the vision, and others only when it is done right. Be willing to fail in order to achieve, and never give up on your vision. Change never comes without resistance.

Often, naysayers just want to pick a fight. They don't want to engage in dialogue. They want you to become a naysayer, too, because then they've won. Follow the advice that has been the mantra of presidential aides for generations: "Never complain, never explain." Just cast vision. Tell positive stories of change and transformation. When people begin to get negative, don't follow them down a path of negativity. Be a "yessayer." At all times, edify.

Also, understand that the complaints of many naysayers are sincere, albeit grumpily expressed. There is often a tendency to, as stated, "confuse Jesus and the horse he rode in on." In other words, confuse the identity of personal faith and the cultural context in which that identity was formed. I like to kindly point out that all we are doing is making the life of faith connect to a newer culture, so that other people can have the same personal, identity-forming faith experiences that the naysayer once had.

# CHAPTER 5
# CONCURRENTLY CULTURAL
# AND COUNTERCULTURAL

Consider professional football. Each year, at the annual draft, someone is awarded the honor of being named Mr. Irrelevant. This dubious title is given to the last player selected. As one might guess, the moniker arose because the last pick in the draft often fails to make the final roster, making the selection irrelevant to the team.

Ironically, the highest relevance for the player is often that they've been selected Mr. Irrelevant. The "winner" gets treated like a king for a week at a festival, banquet, and party. There's a whole cottage industry around the concept, with its own website. They even have an award, called the Lowsman Trophy (that's the opposite of the Heisman Trophy). Instead of the famous running back with extended arm, this trophy features a shocked player dropping the ball.

The idea of relevancy can get a little crazy, in both professional football and in ministry. In the church, some circles strongly emphasize it, while others are stridently opposed to the concept of being relevant. On one hand, there's an entire ministry magazine called *Relevant*. You might guess their opinion. It reflects the relevancy concerns of the seeker movement that has been popular since the 1980s. On the other hand, some might say the recent movement called Emergent could name its magazine (if it had one) Irrelevant, with its emphasis on stepping away from pop culture awareness and its search for new, authentic expressions of faith. This debate extends back through Christian history.

A church that I work closely with experiences the tension of the "relevancy" debate on a regular basis. The pastor is highly interested in relevance. His desire is to break down barriers that prevent people from encountering Jesus. He likes to use language such as, "Our church is a place where you can use 'fun' and 'church' in the same sentence." He also says the people of the congregation are "far from perfect, but they're real." The understated theology is that God is present in the places where we live, as sinful as we may be. This is the essence of the Incarnation. It could be said that the pastor's focus is on the human Jesus—the one who hung out with sinners and tax collectors.

The worship leader, however, is highly interested in what he usually describes as "deeper" worship. He says that his goal is to create a worship environment that enables people to glorify God and know God's presence. In worship, he uses language such as, "Let's enter into a time of worship," and, "Let's give honor and respect to God today." The understated theology is that we as sinful people must cleanse ourselves through faith in Jesus to experience the presence of a God who is without sin and wholly Other. This is the doctrine of sanctification, or to be made holy and set apart for God. It could be said that his focus is on the divine Jesus—the one who became transfigured on the mountaintop.

These may seem like fairly opposite goals and beliefs. In some ways, they are. But these two points of view are not mutually exclusive and can and should coexist in the way the gospel is communicated. For this particular church, it has on occasion created tension. But his church is better off for it. Because of the pastor's and worship leader's unique personalities and passions, the Christian paradox of being cultural and yet countercultural at the same time remains present in this church community.

When a congregation experiences this paradox, it is in a very real way reflecting an ancient tension. At the Council of Chalcedon, in the year 451, the church confessed Jesus as truly man, truly God. Two natures that are in perfect unity. This belief is about as universal as it gets in the Christian church. Although we confess it with our mouths, we often don't show it in our actions. Many churches can't handle the tension and end up focusing just on the human side (being "in the world," or relevant), or just on the divine side (being "not of this world," or conscientiously irrelevant). As R. C. Sproul states,

When we think about the Incarnation, we don't want to get the two natures mixed up and think that Jesus had a deified human nature or a humanized divine nature. We can distinguish them, but we can't tear them apart because they exist in perfect unity.[1]

If the two natures—human and divine—are equally present in Jesus, this means the challenge for those in ministry is to always hold the two in tension: to not get so engrossed in connection that discipleship is lost, or to not get so engrossed in discipleship that the door closes to the world. As a user named Dave commented in the Midnight Oil website reading section,

> We use relevance to the culture to form relationships and do effective evangelism. Then, we build a counter-culture in which people become holy. There is a tension here. I notice that some churches only do cultural relevance. Others only do counter-culture. I so want to hold these in tension. I want to be cultural enough to attract and communicate effectively. I want to be counter-cultural enough to "annoy" people out of complacency and into submission to Christ's sanctifying work in their lives.[2]

In other words, we need to maintain cultural "relevancy" even as we strive to create a Christian culture of discipleship different from the worldly culture at large.

At the church where I got my start in ministry, Ginghamsburg, we experienced a period in which the effort to be relevant surpassed the effort to create a thriving counterculture. We were doing a great job of using cultural language and images to attract people, but the "back door" was almost as big as the "front door." Many people left or stayed mired in their human condition because in our rapid growth we didn't yet have discipleship programs to match evangelistic programs. Ginghamsburg has since shifted the focus of their ministry to an attempt to do both at the same time—to speak with a relevant voice while simultaneously emphasizing discipleship and countercultural living. The church body has grown both spiritually and numerically because of these efforts.

The focus on relevancy to the culture without the balance of creating a counterculture unfortunately has happened a lot in the church, especially during the "seeker" period of the 1980s and 1990s. Out of these movements a newer emphasis on what some call "believer" worship has emerged. Vacillating within the classic tension, the emphasis on the human Jesus is now shifting back toward the divine Jesus.

The use of visual media gets caught in the undertow when it is closely associated with relevant worship and is seen as primarily a tool for outreach. Digital media is not only for outreach purposes. It is true that biblical truth can be expressed in ways that are potentially more enlightening through images relevant to our culture, when compared to images that have long-established meanings in the church. But contrary to what some demonstrate, images may be used for devotion as well. Any single association is false, just as any would be for the printed word. Both are mediums for creating an experience and awareness of God, and are equally valid. This means images are good for worship that strives to be relevant and also good for worship that strives to make disciples. The cultural language of digital media has resonance in both cultural connection and countercultural discipleship.

This marriage of the human and divine languages creates an awareness of the Spirit through which believers and nonbelievers alike can find hope and meaning. The nets are cast much wider when we balance the use of digital media for both outreach and discipleship. It is when we exclude one purpose or the other that the catch is greatly reduced.

If Jesus is both human and divine, and if our goal is to proclaim the Word and make disciples, then we need to be willing to stay near the human Jesus even as we are drawn to the divine Jesus. If we follow the lead of Jesus' ministry on earth, we'll find ourselves striving to communicate in a relevant way through stories and parables that relate to people living in this time. Speaking the language of the culture, or being a Wired Church, means learning how to remain relevant even as we strive to create a counterculture separate and apart from the world.

PART TWO

# DESIGNING MEANINGFUL MEDIA FOR WORSHIP

# CHAPTER 6
# BEYOND THE AV
# MENTALITY

As a Christian who watches television, I find that channel surfing can be a bittersweet experience. On my local digital cable system, there is a cluster of channels just past the kids' channels that qualify as the "spiritual" channels, such as EWTN (the Catholic network), Word (preaching), Trinity Broadcasting Network (televangelism), and Inspiration and PAX-TV ("family" programming). There are also local churches that air their worship services scattered across the spectrum. In spite of an active personal faith, I almost always click right on through these channels without pausing to watch the programming. As far as I can tell, by doing some unscientific polling among other Christians, I am in the majority. It is certainly true that these networks receive low Nielsen ratings, even when compared to other niche networks such as Home and Garden TV or the Animal Planet. Based on the occasional times I do stop and watch, I don't think for the most part it is because of lack of meaningful content or poor production values (well, sometimes the latter). The reason, perhaps, is that most religious television does a poor job of interpreting the gospel to a digital culture. Church television comes across as "churchy" television, an object of parody regardless of the viewer's faith. Much of the programming on these channels still consists of live worship experiences, sermons and theological discussions, and performances by musical groups, which are each forms appropriate to a faithful life but not necessarily fitting in the medium of television.

For years social critics have mocked the efforts of church leaders in media, yet the forms that church television uses continue to look different from the rest of television. It's obvious when you've tuned into religious television, even if the sound is muted and there are no crosses in sight. Regardless of programming decisions to target church or unchurched audiences, if Christian programming fails to reach Christians, it is probably not going to reach the public.

This lack of interpretation in digital media, whether in broadcast television or in local church worship, is what I call the AV mentality. The AV mentality is the use of digital, visual media as an afterthought, an add-on, a value to be added, or something less than an intrinsic ingredient in worship and church life. An AV mentality is one in which the new communication form's primary use is to communicate themes and messages still centrally located, developed, and implemented within old communication forms such as mass print culture. The AV mentality is interested more in documentation than interpretation. Video, audio, and graphics become mere support pieces for the primary communication tool of text. As screens have become assimilated into congregations of all sizes, styles, and theological persuasions, this problem has literally been made visible every Sunday. Simply go to an online retailer such as Worshiphousemedia.com and note that many of the top-selling video clips continue to be abstract shapes and nature footage—pretty eye candy to make the words on screen more noticeable.

Media at its most shallow level is merely illustrative or enhancement. But at a transformational level, media is interpretive, or capable of saying things not possible to say in other forms. Everyone who watches movies understands the difference when they see it. It is the difference between Robert Duvall's performance as an alcoholic who gets on the wagon in *Tender Mercies*, and an Alcoholics Anonymous video on alcoholism. It is the difference between *Shadowlands*, C. S. Lewis's December discovery of relational love as a reflection of God, and my favorite example of how not to reach youth, *SuperChristian*. As noted, literacy at the level of consumption is fairly saturated in this, our third adult generation of electronic media cultural dominance. But understanding the difference at a conceptual level, which is necessary to the development and implementation of effective electronic media ideas, means utilizing a combination of biblical exegesis and storytelling. It means thinking visually. It means the use of story and metaphor.

Digital media are no different from any other medium used to communicate the gospel throughout history, whether that is the scroll, the podium, the pencil, the mimeograph machine, the hot-metal press, or the microphone. Accepting this fact is the key to fully separating media from its messages. For example, a cross mounted in a sanctuary is not an object to be worshiped. Versions of the cross, whether they are wooden or glass or metal, are like stained glass and other media, representative forms for truth as contained in the Scriptures. Although they may be effective communication forms for worship and church life, a projected image of a cross is no more or less intrinsically meaningful than a metal cross or one painted on a canvas. Churches that must have a physical, sculpted cross in the sanctuary may not realize that they are focusing on a representation, however important, of the resurrected Christ, and not on Jesus himself. A cross, hung in a sanctuary, is not *the* cross from Golgotha, and Jesus is not still hung on it.

The screen is the stained glass for the digital age, except now we have the privilege of working in a dynamic rather than a static form. The screen is the ever-changing canvas, constantly transposing new imagery before us. If Pope Gregory persuaded us that icons were the Bible for the illiterate, then the screen is the Bible for the postliterate.

Understandably, church leaders often have a hard time with this transition. For this there are at least two reasons. First, they have been trained differently. Seminaries are bastions of the mass print culture of books and analysis. Most preaching classes, where communication techniques are taught, at our theological seminaries are exercises in exegesis and analysis that often bypass a narrative focus in image, storytelling, and cultural literacy. Most pastors and church leaders who have been seminary trained, no matter what their experience and exposure to digital media culture, must decide after graduation whether to make the radical shift to the presence and use of digital media.

A typical transition for a pastor, preacher, or church leader into digital media initially means continuing to compose sermons without brainstorming groups or digital media accessibility, then finally tacking on AV support to a completed message. Over time, a leader's understanding gradually molts to composing central themes and structural points and then using media to communicate these points, to finally utilizing visual concepts in the conceptual stage of planning. Unfortunately, many leaders never get beyond the first step because it means sharing responsibility of this creative process with others. It means forming creative teams. This is the second reason, giving up complete control of the most powerful icon of a pastor's leadership, the pulpit. (Yet, a team-driven worship service and message, well done, serves to increase the pastor's authority.)

The problem is compounded in the Protestant tradition because the sermon is the core element of the worship experience. But, contrary to what some have suggested, interpreting the gospel to our culture does not mean an abandonment of the sermon as a viable form. And the formation of this new wineskin will occur through replication and adaptation of methodologies already in place in current visual industries and in the arts. Rather, as the sermon mutated from a storytelling to an exegetical experience in the mass print era, it must mutate again, along with other elements of the Christian experience, into a form that speaks to this electronic culture. No one fully knows what this new mutation will completely look like, although there's a good chance it will include images and video, storytelling and participation, and will be much more immersive than its print-age counterpart.

Fortunately for the church, our current digital media system, in the form of film, television, radio, and the Internet, is still prepubescent. Its reputation among some as an isolated, isolating experience fails to take into account the metamorphosis that is occurring as the system matures over hundreds of years into the future. Collaborators produce electronic media. Its creation and ultimately its consumption are meant for groups of people, particularly in relation to the mass print culture of books.

The development of the Internet, as the new media age enters its adolescence, is bearing this out. Business leaders proclaim the arrival of Web 2.0, the dynamic and collaborative descendant of the original, static HTML page. Blogs, vlogs, and the like empower anyone to publish. Everything is networked. Software is becoming a service, not a product. This is even appearing in worship, where innovative churches can ask a survey-style question and get immediate feedback from the congregation through cell phone texting technology.

The future bodes well for those in the church who are willing to move beyond the AV mentality to create electronic media messages that interpret the gospel to, and ultimately transform the listeners of, this new age. The first step in this process is the task of learning to think visually.

# CHAPTER 7
# VISUAL PREACHING AND WORSHIP PLANNING

For most preachers, talking is easy. What is difficult is the conveyance of meaning, or communicating with the right combination of syntax and style to make a message heard. Even with the supposedly captive audience of a congregation the challenge remains, as the expectation for communication has risen along with our digital media options. How do we make our words carry weight? The elephant in the room is that preaching is hard, very hard, and few exhibit a command of oratory, both historically and presently. Some have even said preaching is dead, because so few people practice it well. As noted, the sermon is not dead. It has merely evolved.

While this concept may seem as new as the sudden ubiquity of screens in worship spaces, it is actually a significant part of the Christian tradition. What we call preaching began in a culture of orality with Isocrates and the style of Greek rhetoric—ordered, persuasive arguments that sought to develop and disseminate ideas. By the time of Jesus, amidst the bustle of commerce and new roads in the Hellenistic world, a new medium emerged—the letter. The Apostle Paul saw in letters an opportunity to "mix media" and proclaim the risen Christ using both the established style of rhetoric and the new medium of letters. In fact, some said he was better at the new media than old media (see 2 Corinthians 10:9-10).

The media mix changed over time. With the rise of the mass-printed book and the scientific method, the spoken word came to be regarded as a modification of the written rather than vice versa. Words took on precise, unambiguous meaning. The written word became authoritative. The art of rhetoric was lost and the sermon became a reading.[1]

Now, many worshipers experience a sermon both by hearing it and reading it. Some preachers use a simple bulletin outline; others reprint large portions of their sermon for the congregation to read. Sermons are structured around doctrines and propositions. Arguments are systematic. Words are precise. In fact, the more wedded to book learning the preacher is, the more likely he or she is to carry angst over individual syntactical meaning. Sound familiar?

The irony is that the speaker is much more concerned with individual word choice than the listener is. Largely, listeners today are no longer systematic. The goal is not precision but individual interpretation. Science is being forced to recognize art.

Many of the best speakers in our culture have discovered, like Paul, the power of using a mix of media. Yet the church seems to lag, continuing to trust what is written more than what is heard or seen. Part of such distrust stems from lack of mastery. It is true that creating powerful images and video for worship is hard. Worshipers are sophisticated media consumers, and the expectation of quality is high. (It's paradoxical, however, that expectations remain high even as production values decline with viral Web video and reality television.)

What does all this mean? To be better preachers, we must learn to believe in the power of the visual to proclaim Christ. We must move beyond just text and learn to think also in image, discovering the power of mixing visual media into our preaching. Here are some suggestions for integrating visual language into preaching and worship.

# FROM INFORMATION TO INTERPRETATION

Video as a medium informs (provides focus) and persuades (provides hope), but the former is a function of the latter. Video is primarily a persuasive medium. It is best used to convey an idea with emotion. As a multisensory form, digital media has more physiological power than any single form individually. Video by itself is multimedia because it combines images and sound.

Despite what I heard in school, in this post-*Network* age it is difficult to argue that there is objectivity in any form of media. The gatekeeping function of mass media is now assumed. Television news, by its very clipped nature, forces opinion and editorial comment. Watch the lead story of the six o'clock news on three different channels to see what I mean. O. J. Simpson looked a lot less like a criminal on the cover of *Newsweek* than he did on *Time*. Without placing political or ethical judgments on the gate-keepers, it is easy to realize that the bite is the essence of this form.

In this context, information is best suited to text. This means that during announcement time in worship, tell the story on video and give the details in the bulletin. And during the administrative board meeting, visually introduce to whom the money is going, and give the figures in the line chart that can be analyzed.

Using digital media in a multisensory environment means saying the same thing that is being said in other media, but in a unique way. This is the nonlinear approach.

Don't try to visualize content that is best communicated orally. If you've painted a word picture in a sermon, don't settle for putting up that picture. Let the oral medium do its thing, and then do the visual thing: say the same thing a different way. To illustrate Jesus' parable of the man and his bigger barns (Luke 12:13-21), you might create a series of images in which sections of a house are added sequentially: the suburban real estate deal being the Baby Boomer version of more grain.

In planning event media, continually ask, what things work best for graphics or video? What cannot be said another way? Watch late-night TV for one week, especially the parts before it turns into a talk show. How do Leno, Letterman, and Conan engage the audience visually? Do they use video clips, and if so, what do they say? How do they work?

How might a teaching be interpreted to digital media? Many church-based educational curricula are developed around a book or a series of studies. Video might be used to support an argument presented in the text, or used to set up a theme or a metaphor for the argument. Research on the Internet can reveal quantitative information about cultural attitudes, or historical responses relating to the argument. There are many possibilities. Education in digital culture is much more "object-based." A curriculum might consist of many different objects of varying communication forms: a book, a video and study guide for storytelling to and within the group, audiotapes for reflection later, use of the Internet, or an on-location video illustrating or interpreting the theme.

## Address the Visual Style of the Intended Audience

Use visual cues from culture as the basis for sermon planning. This helps you learn to think in image. When planning, don't just start with a blank computer or a pen and paper. Try to immerse yourself in the visual culture around you. Make it a part of your everyday routine.

Many preachers are hesitant to use "target audience" thinking in identifying for whom a sermon is being preached. There is fear that some people feel left out. But the idea that a preacher can reach "everyone" is a myth. It's impossible to reach everyone. There are metaphors that will have a general appeal for some listeners and a very specific appeal for others. In other words, some will find deeper levels of meaning in any particular metaphor, while others have little personal connection to it.

For example, there was broad appeal and connection found in a "ripple" metaphor. As producers, we saw people connecting to God through the act of dropping rocks into a pond as a symbol of creating their own ripples of Christ's love in the world. Afterward one worshiper expressed that this was the most meaningful service he had ever experienced. He then went on to tell us that he is a physics professor. The metaphor of ripples had a very specific appeal for him because physics is something he is passionate about. And although others also found meaning in this service, they may not have made the same deep connections.

Andrew Bear posted in an online seminar that there's an evangelistic component to visual preaching: "If you are trying to connect with a particular microculture, what images do they immerse themselves in? What movies are connecting with them, and what images are in those movies? What music do they listen to, and what is the style of design on the album covers?" While this insight is helpful, understand there is also not much of a difference between the cultural tastes of the typical churchgoer and the typical nonchurchgoer. The culturally much-maligned notion of the evangelical megachurch that creates multimedia experiences for evangelistic worship doesn't tell the whole story. This isn't just for the unchurched or seeker person. We all live in the same digital culture.

For example, on Pentecost a lot of people use the passage from Acts 2 that includes "tongues as of fire." Whether seeker or churched person, this is simply a creepy concept. Flaming tongues hanging from the ceiling? Seminary graduates and church insiders often forget that this image needs decoding. Image can help, but not images of tongues. The most famous cultural tongue is the Rolling Stones logo, which is probably not the association a sermon on Pentecost wants to make. An outsider mentality is needed to evaluate all communication happening at the church on Pentecost.

## Immerse Yourself in Visual Culture

I worked with another congregation on their "worship presentation." One Sunday morning the church's worship producer asked me to listen closely to the sermon. She was concerned that the preacher's message on alcohol and drugs was too heavy-handed.

My response: it was information, sensitively portrayed—but information that may or may not have any impact. A person dealing with addiction probably already knows such information but is helpless to stop her or his behavior. For someone being tempted, such information is no match for the desire to feel good. So what is a preacher to do? What alternative option is there to the time-honored Christian tradition of using information as a scare tactic?

Consider *Munich*, Steven Spielberg's recent reflection on revenge. In this film, an Israeli agent goes on a mission to hunt down and kill those responsible for the terror act at the Munich Olympic Games in 1972. While many have focused on the political layers in the film, there is also a strong spiritual layer. The story is about the agent losing his soul as he hunts down those responsible. Once he learns the carnal knowledge of murder, he cannot unlearn it. He cannot go back. Herein lies a meaningful sermon on the abuse of drugs, alcohol, or any other "illicit" act. The danger is that we can lose our soul. We can learn things that we then wish we had never learned. We want to return to innocence that we can no longer experience. The high leaves and we are left with a haunting. (Johnny Cash captured this well in his final hit song before he died, "Hurt.")

The power of this realization isn't in information. Information isn't bad; it just can't hold a candle to the glimpse of reality that one experiences when watching a movie like *Munich*. To preach such a message is to shift from a sermon based on the written word to a sermon based on the visual word.

The idea of learning to think in image is a plea to discover the power of art to communicate the gospel. Give listeners more than information. Give them an experience of God through image and story that will open their eyes and help them discover why Truth is so true.

So you don't have to be a creative genius. Just remember two things: (1) be a student of the culture and (2) be adaptable. A student of the culture is one who is constantly in tune with techniques and trends in TV, film, and the Internet. Put down this book for a while and turn on the tube. More than just a couch potato, though, a student of the culture watches TV critically. As you surf, pay more attention to the commercials than the programming. The thirty-second ads contain the true innovation. Where else will a company spend millions of dollars for the opportunity to spend less than a minute convincing you to purchase their product? Sounds crazy, but we know it's true. And to pull it off, they hire producers who understand how to speak the language. There's no better lab anywhere.

It has been noted that television advertising is declining in the age of TiVo and the Internet. This reality is just making marketers savvier (and maybe more desperate) in their creations. Find a major national ad campaign that appeals to you visually. Then note over the next few weeks all of the places you see the campaign appear, from traditional advertising media such as television, magazines, and billboards to fresh media such as YouTube videos and MySpace templates. As digital culture spreads horizontally, the means to communicate to the culture follows suit, and the advertising companies are at the forefront of figuring out how.

However, remember that fluency means both adapting media trends and making media trends. One trend is the pace rule. Never take too long to say any one thing; as a rule, keep the camera moving, because we are the attention-deficit generation.

The flip side of that, however, is the old-fashioned idea of anticipation. The most effective media may be that which, within the quickened pace, enables us to pause and reflect for a moment. Cameron Crowe, director of *Jerry Maguire*, used a long pause in the midst of a fast-paced film to increase anticipation for the love interests to kiss. He says, "Reflect. Don't let Hollywood dictate the influence on culture. Move to the lead, then pass it." Of course, being able to effectively set new standards requires a strong grasp of the existing standards.

While surfing channels one afternoon early in my career, I came across a show called *Bill Nye the Science Guy* on the local PBS affiliate. This show excelled at portraying complex concepts of science in easily understood ways to reach youth by using a combination of humor, graphics, and heavily treated video. I thought, how can the unique Bill Nye concept be used in a ministry context? The result for me was a call-to-worship video that illustrated the concept of a "capstone," a biblical metaphor which is no longer part of our everyday culture, in easy to understand ways.

To be adaptable means to redeem an idea for use in a ministry context. Shaky text was a big trend in video that stemmed from the credit roll of the film *Se7en* (1996). Although the movie itself, about a serial killer that takes his modus operandi from the seven deadly sins, is dark and I don't recommend it, the opening credit roll struck me in its powerful use of imagery and text that couldn't sit still. The text treatment from that film was intended to create a state in which the very frame itself, the foundation of the picture, was about to come apart in chaos. I appreciated the chaos treatment, and decided to adapt it to a TV spot for local multi-market cable for Christmas.

The spot contrasted the chaos of busy lives to the peace and presence of the Christ Child. Of course, no one knew that this video spot was referenced from such a dark source. Some metaphors are redeemable.

An excellent way to track visual thoughts is to keep a storyboard journal. Get a small bound notebook, or use the pad on your mobile device, and draw a dozen or so 4"x3" rectangles. Leave it next to your remote. When you see inspiring ads, sketch them out. This will become a handy reference for conceptualizing video later.

For more information and ideas for thinking creatively, see the section in part 3 on building creative teams (page 91).

## Understand Visual Metaphor

There is great power in metaphor. Most preachers confine metaphorical language to an illustration for an individual talking point. There might be three to four metaphors over the course of a sermon. While this method may work in literate-based preaching, it isn't conducive to visual interpretation. The visual preacher understands the power of a single visual metaphor. The use of image is the mechanism for persuasion in this culture, just as rhetoric was the mechanism for persuasion in a preliterate culture.

Also, be aware that *metaphor* isn't a catchall word for anything visual. Preachers should be able to sum up how the idea connects with a metaphor in a few words by completing this sentence: this biblical story/concept/ message is like _____ (insert a visual idea). For example, belief without the disciplines of prayer and study is like fast-food faith. This will help ensure that an image is actually a visual metaphor and not a textual one. More on metaphor coming up in the next chapter.

## Be Nonlinear

Every human creature is creative. To harness the creative spirit given by God is to become nonlinear. It means not sticking to the subject. It means that the random thoughts that pop into your head at odd times, like during prayer, may not be odd at all but rather part of the work of the creative Spirit. A nonlinear thinker recognizes and allows these thoughts to happen and is bold enough to verbalize them to others.

Don't just exegete text and then find image to match; be willing to let image exist and grow developmentally along with text. Think about visual references in culture to communicate ideas. Exegete culture along with scripture. If there is a metaphor to go with a theme, spend time exegeting the metaphor.

One weekend a team I was on team brainstormed the image of ripples in a pond to describe the relationship of Jesus to his disciples described in John 15:9-15. While the preacher, Tim Coombs, loved the concept, when he sat down to develop his sermon, he found himself following the usual exegetical pattern and ignoring the image. So, instead, he searched the term *ripples* on the Internet. Instantly he had dozens of websites explaining the physics of waves and energy transfer. There was more to say with theological and cultural resonance than time would allow.

## Focus on a Single Idea and Find an Image that Communicates It

Many people who attend worship find it hard to recall the sermon later in the week. Even the most gifted preachers may leave worshipers with only one memorable point, scripture reference, or illustration to retain in their memories after the service ends.

In an effort to improve retention, a lot of pastors turn to the use of image and PowerPoint presentations as a sort of "visual aid" to their sermons. Often, though, nothing changes in the level of listener recall. Images too often are visual imprints of the same words that are printed in the bulletin. Listeners still are left with one particular scripture, sermon point, or illustration.

How can preachers design sermons with image in mind? First, look for a central image that communicates the idea or theme for the entire worship service. Carefully choosing a single thematic image gives pastors an avenue for connecting ideas with a common thread. Once the singular focus for the day has been decided, all aspects of worship can be built on variations of that common visual theme.

Scripture and sermon points then become visual without going in several different directions. Retention improves when this communication technique is employed. The "theme and variations approach" to visual images narrows the focus and effectiveness of a message. As authors Andy Stanley and Ronald Jones note, "Every message should have one central idea, application, insight, or principle that serves as glue to hold the other parts together."[2]

Andrew Bear also said during our online seminar, "Something that I experience as I pray with a scripture and what God wants to say to this people is that often an image will come to me. I try to create that image, with the limited time and resources I have, as a main symbol for the sermon. So it's kind of a spiritual thing. An image comes, not with words attached, but just an image. It's almost revelatory."

Further, the image needs to be present throughout worship and established long before the sermon begins. It is important to help people see the connections between the biblical truth and the visual representation of it throughout worship. In many of the services we've visited as consultants and as worshipers, there has been a disconnect between the visual representation of the gospel and the spoken or musical representation of it. It's important to help worshipers interpret the images used in worship. It is not helpful to simply project images with no attempt at a verbal connection. A person should be able to walk into worship at any point in the service and quickly understand the image.

## Brainstorm Sermon Images with a Trusted Small Group

If we are truly the body of Christ, why not practice it when designing worship? Group or team worship design is an opportunity to come together and make the most of collective gifts, knowledge, and experience. Everything, including music, media, and (especially) sermons, can benefit from the brainstorming and critique of a small, diverse group of designers.

Brainstorming is a technique best used in small groups in which random thoughts and responses are verbalized from a seed thought surrounding a particular topic. In brainstorming, there is no bad idea; all ideas are valid and noted. Brainstorming can be long and messy. It requires the total trust of all players. It also takes time to develop. Teams that have been together a few months are much more effective at brainstorming and generating creative energy and ideas than a team that has just begun.

Further, one does not need to be a creative genius. The number-one rule for creativity: there is nothing new under the sun, and we have known that for thousands of years. For example, Western pop culture has become so self-aware, it is now meta-culture; it is continually regurgitating itself. Think, for example, of the mashup concept discussed above. Some say that the age of the multimedia database has stifled innovation because performers have had the work of other performers always before them. I think it is the other way around. This age has democratized art. Now everyone has access to fine art forms formerly reserved for higher socioeconomic classes with leisure time. But, instead of sustaining these traditional forms, the culture has created something out of its own experience. Imagery that sets trends has lost the tag of "fine" and has become "pop." Fine art connoisseurs say the latter isn't even art at all; it is too common. But that is the beauty of it, and it is a reflection of the God-image with which each human is born. This meta-state is not a bad thing. Out of so much borrowing is rising a new form of creative experience that gleans from a higher digital media literacy, using the same creative ideas packaged in fresh ways. Digital media is giving each of us the chance to become artists. You don't need a professional on your team.

## Expect a Learning Curve

As in Paul's admonition to the Corinthians that they must first drink milk, not eat solid food, it takes developmental time for creating effective media in worship and education. It takes time to master speaking in a totally different language. When I first began meeting with senior pastor Mike Slaughter at Ginghamsburg Church for the purpose of integrating media into his sermon, he would preach his sermon to me, and then say, "Okay, what can you give me?" It wasn't an environment conducive to creativity at that time. I suggested that we bring in a couple of other people to create a team atmosphere to help stimulate visual ideas. Even Mike, who had used multi-image slide projectors as a youth pastor in the 1970s, had an understanding of digital media, but still had a learning curve while adapting to preaching out of this new form. Preaching has now become transformed into a convergence of sensory experiences that combine images, video, film, and sounds alongside litanies, repetition, and exegesis. Expect a learning curve in teaching and preaching, which authority and tradition have long protected; this learning to let go is just as crucial as the process of learning a new cultural idiom.

## Expect to Spend Some Money, but Not Too Much

The cost of learning a new cultural language in a community is often cited as a barrier to change. However, the early adopters have taught us how to become adept at funding the process on a shoestring.

During my years in seminary, my wife pursued her music degrees at Wright State University, a local state-funded institution. Those were lean years. Much of the money I made to keep going was from contract media work that came from people associated with the seminary. The experience taught me a number of solutions to computer issues, but more importantly it taught me that there is always an affordable solution to a problem, even if nobody knows what it is yet. That rule has served me well in learning to speak the language of media in church life.

Funding issues invariably fade away when you ask the "So what?" question. How does the use of media enhance someone's experience of Jesus? How does it point them toward the person of Christ? If it is not helping persons serve God and love their neighbors, then you might be looking at a "gee whiz—look what we can do!" purpose for the resources, and that is poor stewardship. Media is simply a communication form for Christian truth, which builds community (a common language) among those who are committed to the good news of Jesus Christ.

# CHAPTER 8
# BASICS FOR BUILDING VISUAL ELEMENTS

In this chapter we get inside the practical tactics that are used by a media minister. These include guidelines for video production and how to use visual metaphor. Though the subject of metaphor might sound like the pursuit of a literary critic who reviews printed novels, it is actually the bedrock tactic for media ministry.

## THE METAPHOR

The metaphor is the single most important element of media ministry design.

The metaphor is not the theme. The theme is a functional description of the primary message that is to be shared. For a Sunday morning it might be God's grace, or for a discipleship class it might be God's covenant. The metaphor is how the theme is to be communicated so that it can be understood or at least embodied through experience.

The metaphor is a tangible representation of an abstract idea. The Bible depends heavily upon metaphors. Every major theme represented in Scripture is communicated through metaphor. The Holy Spirit is a dove, the call of God is heard in the ordinary burning bush, God's covenant is sealed in the rainbow. Metaphors abound in the Bible because they are the essence of oral communication. Prophets such as Jeremiah spoke of a potter and his clay to represent God's continued relationship with an unrepentant Israel, and Zechariah talked about a flying scroll in an apocalyptic vision in which God sends out a curse rebuking the captive Israelites for not keeping the Law. Even in the early church, leaders realized the value of the metaphor. Clement of Alexandria advocated the use of symbols such as doves, fish, a musician's lyre, an anchor, or a "ship running before the wind."[1]

As you explore what it means to be a Wired Church, read the Bible as a communication document. Notice all the times and ways God uses creative communications in indigenous language to lead God's people.

The metaphor may be a phrase or an entire sentence, but it is often object-oriented, or at least a combination of text and object. Metaphors are all around us, but we notice that a metaphor is "dead" when it is overused (trite) or becomes a function of literal speech. In his parables Jesus used familiar objects, the staples of an agrarian society: a mustard seed, a woman with a broom, workers in a field, yeast, a banquet feast, and so on. In seeking the metaphor, ask the question, to what does the theme compare? What are the contemporary, dynamic equivalents to Jesus' agrarian examples? Again, the theme is an analytical, propositional, or functional description. You pursue the metaphor through the imagination of what it is and how it is to be told.

Metaphors are vital for a number of reasons. They make abstract concepts more easily understood, thereby increasing retention. More important, according to Mark 4, the use of metaphor was Jesus' model for public ministry.[2]

Don't give up on applying metaphors. It is not always easy, especially when working with persons who are conditioned to create themes in propositional and abstract form, which is the methodology of the print culture. But time and again I have seen that the effectiveness of a presentation is directly determined by the effectiveness of the metaphor that communicates the theme. For more on metaphor, see our *Design Matters: Creating Powerful Imagery for Worship* (Abingdon Press, 2006).

# EXPANDING THE PALETTE: TWENTY-ONE WAYS TO USE MEDIA IN WORSHIP

Known for his quirky laid-back style and affinity for "happy little trees," Bob Ross, public television's most famous oil painter, had an almost hypnotic presence as he created picturesque landscapes and nature scenes. Bob's soft-spoken voice and unique witticisms were only one part of what made him so mesmerizing. His ability to create whole environments completely from scratch with no photo references made you want to watch.

Bob's name may or may not go down in history alongside Picasso, Michelangelo, and Dali, but observing his paintings and techniques can draw in even the most uninterested party. Those who have seen his show may have noticed that he had a whole arsenal of paints and brushes at his disposal. Ross never just painted with one or two colors. He used his entire palette to create all kinds of interesting variations on color that, once applied to the canvas, matched perfectly.

Rather than using one or two types of videos or images as an ongoing practice, media ministers can create a visually rich experience in worship with a wide palette of material that varies from week to week. For instance, most churches with screens project song lyrics, and most understand that images behind the lyrics are better than solid colors. Others use movie clips on a regular basis, which can be very effective.

But there is much more that can be done. The following list of media types and uses will help you expand your media palette in worship. They are listed alphabetically by graphics and video. Note that this list isn't meant to be comprehensive.

## Graphic Images

### 1. Announcement Graphics

Many congregations like to run a looping stream of still images before and after worship. The model is similar to what one encounters sitting in a theater, waiting for the movie to start.

Such loops can be an effective complement to a more complete promotional strategy. The tendency, however, is for them to become "wall candy." When creating announcement loops, use humor, and vary the images as much as possible from week to week.

Announcement images can be a good project for beginning graphic artists. It is also one of many venues through which a congregation can effectively create a visual brand for specific ministries and events.

### 2. Illustration Graphics

Illustrations are a great way to make a point, drive the message home, or just get a good laugh. If possible, create at least two or three image-based illustrations for every sermon. It helps keep the pace going and breaks up oral monotony. This requires some degree of planning with the preacher, usually in going over sermon notes together during the week.

Funny illustrations can get a great response, such as featuring the pastor's face in a variety of silly settings or through photo manipulation.

They can also be stunning magazine photos, newspaper clippings, or other images that are poignant reminders of what's going on in the world. One Sunday afternoon a pastor went home and read the newspaper. As he was flipping through the pages he saw an ad for a BMW car that caught his attention. Being a former owner of a BMW, he was still an interested fan and took the time to read about the latest features. After perusing the ad for a while, he was taken aback when his eye caught an image of a malnourished child from Sudan adorning the opposite page. It stopped him in his tracks, and it was cause for contemplation. This experience led to an illustration the following week in which the pastor talked, and the screen illustrated how we are often more aware of the "Sedans" in our lives than the "Sudans." It was a very moving and memorable moment, and as he later told me, the basis for a dramatic shift in the ministry of the congregation.

## 3. Main Image

If you want people who come to worship to "get it" and take "it" home with them, creating a single image that represents the metaphor, and thus the theme, for the day can be very helpful.

Ideally, this main image would be displayed even before worship starts. It would appear in between songs, before and after videos and movie clips, and any other time there isn't another images that makes sense. It is also very useful as a visual cue once the pastor has moved on from a particular scripture or sermon point. Consider it a default image: rather than going to black or another random image when there is nothing else new to project, go to your main image for the day.

To really drive home the visual theme, consider placing it on the front of your program or bulletin for the day. It's less expensive and a lot cooler than "cheesy" bulletin clipart.

## 4. Scripture Graphics

Most budding designers think of text when they think about scripture on the screen. While text laid out well can be a nice way to present scripture, there's a much more powerful and enlightening way to handle scripture. Find an element, character, or environment present in any given scripture and illustrate it with an image on the screen, without ever typing a character. It becomes the visual representation of the scripture to communicate in tandem with the written (bulletin and Bible) and spoken forms.

When given the task to illustrate the story of Philip and the Ethiopian eunuch on the road to Jerusalem, Jason created an image of a long road stretching off to a city on the horizon. The single image captured the story in a much more effective way than simply spilling the story's text from Acts on the screen (creating a bouncing-ball effect where worshipers follow each word as it is spoken).

## 5. Sermon Points

This one is both still and moving.

Beyond putting the exact text on the screen that is in the bulletin, a speaker's main points might be illustrated with still graphics, or 2-D and 3-D animations.

Brief videos may be combined with graphic images to create moving type, for example. Also, with the capability, "lower-thirds," or the combination of live camera shots with graphic images, provide reinforcement of a concept while leaving the preacher's face on the screen.

## 6. Sermon Series

Many pastors like to preach sermons in series. This can be both good and bad when it comes to media. It's fairly common for churches to use the same main graphic for the entire series. This can become quite repetitive; usually, after the second week the congregation will begin to ignore the image on the screen.

Using the same image can also make the series feel like it isn't progressing. Even if the pastor is bringing new ideas to the pulpit each week, if none are being brought to the screen, people can feel as though things are going nowhere. It's important to keep in mind that, in terms of communication forms, the screen is both ubiquitous and dominant. It often overshadows what is being spoken, for good or bad, so it's extremely important to make the visuals progress too.

There are a couple of ways to keep the screen as fresh as the preaching during a series (assuming, of course, the preaching is fresh each week). First, you might consider creating variations on the theme graphic for the series. Make each week look similar, but alter the design enough to make it stand on its own.

Next, you might give each week its own metaphor or unique theme but have an overall series graphic, icon, color, or typeface that ties them together.

A church Jason served did a series called Divine Direction where each week featured a different direction-themed metaphor. The individual weeks were True North (a compass metaphor), Personal Navigator (GPS), Go West (cowboy riding off into the sunset), and Direction Unexpected (moss growing on the north side of trees). Each week had its own look that kept momentum going and people engaged.

### 7. "Slide Show" Graphic Sequences

Commonly used for feature music, openers, drama, storytelling, and closers, these sequences are good for illustrating ideas presented through other mediums. This is a common use of media in many congregations—for example, a youth mission trip might be highlighted through a slideshow of snapshots set to live music.

## Videos

### 8. Announcement Videos

Make boring announcements fun with short videos highlighting upcoming events in the life of the church. Many churches beginning to use video start here. They are a great way to exercise some creativity in worship and aren't threatening to people leery of media.

For style tips, reference simple but effective broadcast commercials. For example, one church was having a food drive and wanted to let the congregation know in a way that would make a lasting impression. They created a spoof of a *Saturday Night Live* sketch in which two guys rapped about canned food and parking lots. It was a riot, yet it also contained all of the information people would need to participate. It was followed up by a live announcement from the stage to reiterate the particulars of how the drive would work.

Another church parodies the *Saturday Night Live* "Weekend Update" using a simple voice-over and still images over a cityscape background.

If possible, try to follow up the video announcement with a spoken word. Sometimes people get caught up in the experience of the video announcement and miss all of the information. Using multiple media for the message is much more effective.

Announcement videos external to the church might also fall under the media minister's responsibility, such as producing a 30-second TV spot advertising a Christmas campaign.

### 9. B-roll behind the Speaker

It's just like your local news. "B-roll" is a term for the background footage with or without sound that plays while an anchor reads the story on air. B-roll comes from the B-reel, or the cutaway reel in editing suites. This might be news footage from the local station, environmental shots establishing a locale or setting, or shots of a person, event, or place. It can reinforce the power of a preacher's message without taking the energy to go somewhere else in a sermon.

A preacher wanted to talk about a local college basketball star who had tragically died in a car accident. We called a network affiliate in town, and they were happy to provide a minute of footage of the young man on the court, which we ran during the sermon while the preacher talked about what had happened.

In spite of the sterile title and reference point in the world of news, judicious use of b-roll can be very evocative. In the ripples service mentioned earlier, we showed a couple of minutes of recorded footage of rocks hitting a pond and creating ripples, while a soft soundtrack played underneath. The footage was very simple, a single shot created by the pastor on his home camera. It created a powerful, emotional moment.

### 10. Countdown Videos

3 . . . 2 . . . 1 . . . worship! Countdowns are "lead-ins," with a real-time counter embedded in the video, used to literally count down the minutes and seconds until worship begins. Any video prior to the "official" time is a great way to draw in people who tend to straggle in slowly to worship. Countdowns are great for social butterflies, as they give people warning to end their conversations and train them to realize that worship has a definite beginning point. The catch, however, is that you have to actually start the service as soon as the counter reaches zero!

### 11. Drama Setup Videos

Drama can be a very effective way to share the message in a different creative form. While many churches don't have a budget large enough to build elaborate sets, most have screens. Rather than relying on physical sets alone, consider creating a video introduction to your drama.

One Easter we created a drama in which three guys find themselves on the side of the road, where their truck has just broken down. We didn't have the means to drive a truck on stage, so we created a video introduction with the three guys driving down the road when their truck begins to sputter. They stop, open the hood, and smoke pours out, filling the screen. In the live setting, at the appropriate time, we blasted "smoke" (dry ice, which can be created inexpensively with a small machine from a party supply store) onto stage left. The same guys entered through the cloud, making the transition from screen to stage seamless. It was the prefect setup!

## 12. Dramas on Video

A lot of congregations beginning to use video will try to create video-based dramas. This is actually very difficult to achieve, as the medium is hard on actors, and other elements such as lighting and sound have dramatic impact on production quality. Many congregations don't realize how difficult it is to basically create a short film. Usually, the "cheese factor" is pretty high.

## 13. "Live" Satellite Videos

If you're in a large church with multiple simultaneous services or other special activities going on, you might consider cutting to someone on camera (a roving reporter) somewhere else on campus to show other ministries in action.

One church Jason visited had a weekend called "Blessing of the Bikes" where motorcyclists from all over the area rode choppers in to be prayed over. During the announcement time, the person on stage giving the announcements "spoke" (via faux satellite) with an associate pastor who was out with the bikes. It was a creative way to let people know what was going on that day outside, during, and after worship.

## 14. Looping Video or Animations

Loops can be effective before, during, and after worship; behind song lyrics and featured music; and most anywhere that you want to add to the visual experience. Their most popular use is behind song lyrics in the service, but they can be particularly useful when used before worship to set up the theme or provide ambient eye candy as people enter the sanctuary.

## 15. Mission Moments

Labeled in various ways, this type of video is a one- to two-minute interview and montage that highlights various activities in the life of the congregation. For reference, think about a local news segment featuring a reporter's voice, sound bites from people on the scene, and footage to illustrate. (In industry terms, these are called "packages.")

People don't want to give to pay the utilities as much as they want to give to fund "frontline" ministry where lives are changed. (Of course, paying the light bill enables more visible ministries to happen, but that's another story.) Showing a video that features the real-world efforts of a congregational ministry can generate enthusiasm and giving far beyond a long-winded description of the same activity from behind the pulpit.

At a church we served, mission moments became so popular and frequent that we created a special *bumper*, which is a term for a short transitional segment of video that is often driven by motion effects and animation. This same bumper opened every mission moment video, which effectively branded the idea of missions to the congregation. After a while we got sick of the same opener so we began to create thematically specific introductions with the same name, "Mission Moment," such as a hammer and wood title sequence for a Mission Moment of a Habitat for Humanity house-building project.

### 16. Movie Clips

This is the prefect solution for many churches, ranging from a fledgling ministry with no money to a church with vast resources. Bring in millions of dollars in production value to your church for the cost of a rental. Relevant film clips from Hollywood studios can bring immediacy to any message. And by relevant, we mean resonant, not just current. An older film with just the right story can capture a congregation in both context and memory just as well, if not better, than the latest new release.

Coming up with good film clip ideas can be the challenge. There have been a number of books published that are full of clip ideas, such as the Videos That Teach series and Blockbuster Movie Illustrations. Subscription-based websites such as http://www.movieministry.com, http://www.wing-clips.com, and http://www.screenvue.com are also helpful.

Our new favorite search method is to use the Movie Keyword Analyzer at the Internet Movie Database (http://www.imdb.com). Simply type a word such as *compass* in the search field and then click on the keyword result that comes up. As of this writing, compass brought up fifteen movies with good potential, such as *Out of Africa, The Client, Message in a Bottle*, and more.

Often, the best source is a movie buff sitting next to you in a worship design meeting.

Use, but don't abuse, film clips. Keep them fresh and not typical. Avoid reuse. A well-placed film clip ignites many services, but like anything else, weekly use will kill its spark.

### 17. "On the Street" Videos

A format that has been around a long while but made popular (again) on late night television, these are an effective way to set up a theme and get a feel for real-world opinion on a topic. A detailed description of how to create an "On the Street" video can be found in the Bonus Materials accompanying this book at www.thewiredchurch2.com.

### 18. Scripture Videos

These are visual representations of scripture and can be driven by voice-over, text on the screen, or both. Break out of the "scripture reading" rut and present the same stories in another medium. It will likely make the Bible more connectional for your congregation. This is a favorite of ours because it brings biblical story into contemporary worship (as opposed to single, "proof-text" verses extracted from their context to prove doctrines and concepts).

### 19. Testimony Videos

As stated earlier, testimonies are great for compressing a long faith story from the community into a concise summary, with the added emotional benefit of music and images to illustrate. They can also make people sound more articulate than they really are (anyone who has ever squirmed through an interminable live testimony in worship can appreciate that).

As a rule of thumb, aim for about a two-minute video with three parts: Act 1, thrity to forty-five seconds of what happened prior to their faith encounter; Act 2, thirty to forty-five seconds of what transpired to make their heart become "strangely warmed," and turn to God; and Act 3, thirty seconds or so of what has happened since. Between the three parts can appear transitional elements with graphics and text describing the basic ideas in brief, visual form.

### 20. Theme/Metaphor Setup Videos

Think of these as digital parables. These are personal favorites. Usually, they are short and are not designed to stand on their own but rather as part of a multisensory experience in which many different elements all work together to communicate a single idea. For example, a service about direction, using a compass metaphor, can use a spinning compass video to begin worship.

21. Transition Video/Animations

One of the keys to worship that connects to the digital culture is moving away from a linear format where one element ends, then another begins, often after an excruciating 20- to 30-second pause in which whatever awareness of the Holy Spirit the congregation has is lost. More tightly connected worship flows create the sense of one seamless worship experience. One of the best ways to achieve this is by overlapping elements and using visual imagery to fill gaps. Videos and animations lasting fifteen to thirty seconds can bridge from one element to another, creating a smooth worship experience.

In the industry, these are called "bumpers." For reference, think about the short pieces with the corporate logo that come up during commercial breaks on network television. The same thing can be done in worship. Even better than the church logo, however, is using a thematic element for the day. This transforms what was once a negative gap in between other elements in worship into a new and different way to further communicate the main idea.

# PRODUCING VIDEO: THE PRINCIPLES

After you have chosen a genre for your ministry clip, there are five critical principles for producing incredible ministry video:

## 1. Content Is King

I frequently read trade magazines to stay abreast of creative and technical innovation in the media ministry. Often, I am struck by advances in technology that precede gaps in the communication process. This intuition was confirmed one day when I received a trade magazine issue with a byline in big type that read "Content Is King!"

Of course, content is king, the most important aspect of the production. Don't get a misplaced determination of the importance of a clip because of its production value. Ask the "So what?" question at least three times over the course of planning and producing a video clip.

Variations of the question include:

a) What if we don't show it?
b) What is it really saying, and how well does the video communicate?
c) How does it add to the experience of the event?

Novice producers tend to get caught up in the random, meaningless, deadly use of visual effects. One example is the use of video for messages that are not central to the event, because it reinforces to participants the confusion between the medium and its assumed messages of entertainment. Great media tells powerful, life-changing stories. It is conceived, planned, and implemented as a critical component of worship and discipleship. Like any other medium, it should not be used unless it is central to the experience of God.

## 2. An Effective Graphic or Video Clip Makes One Point

Don't try to accomplish too much through a single media element, which is most effective when it communicates a single message, in a language that the listener can understand. (However, don't be surprised if the videotaped metaphor means different things to various persons, exceeding even what the creator intended.)

I made this mistake as a student. I had contracted to produce a promotional video for a student ministry organization at a local state school, Wright State University. The video was intended to (a) excite local churches about transforming the lives of college-age students, (b) increase funding for student-focused ministries, and (c) recruit students to be a part of the organization. Obviously (c) did not go with (a) or (b), and I was unable to establish the "point" of the piece.

The now clichéd business axiom, Less Is More, applies. Digital culture has shortened our attention span. Now we all collectively have attention deficit disorder. Choose one central theme and explore it. Breadth is bad; depth is good. Depth may also be achieved through the use of other media. Depth is the purpose of multimedia. For example, a teaching series could use the video clip for a testimony, a printed guide for the study, classroom discussion as interactivity, and a hunt via a web browser for more information on a subject.

## 3. Keep the Big Picture

Ever notice how easy it is to get so involved in the creative process that you forget what it is like to be the viewer? A proper perspective helps reorient the important and not-so-important details of a production. One viewer perspective is that shorter is always better. Good rules of thumb for program length are:

- Announcements and worship video pieces: one to one and a half minutes.
- Feature worship/event pieces: two to three minutes.
- Nonworship program pieces for education and small group applications: three to five minutes.

## 4. Video Is for Persuasion, Not Information

Visual images do not analyze. They tell stories. Therefore all video is persuasive because it requires multiple hooks to have an impact on the senses. With music and voice-over, videos inspire the senses. Information that needs to be communicated, then, often is best done in multiple forms. Movie trailers at the theater prior to a film or at home with surround sound get viewers excited. Those same viewers know, though, that to get information about the film, the best method is to check on the Internet, look in the newspaper, or call the box office. There is a distinct difference between informative and persuasive mediums. Video is persuasive in that it establishes the setting and creates emotional connections, drawing viewers to a point of action, which may then be communicated in more detail through text.

## 5. Not All Video Is Created Equal

Clips serve different purposes at different times. Sometimes a little piece is more appropriate as a support mechanism, and at other times a stand-alone piece is more appropriate. In worship, support pieces may introduce a character or situation that is then acted out in live fashion, through drama, monologue, testimony, or music. In other situations a story is best communicated in a feature fashion, which stands alone.

CHAPTER 9

# A QUICK GUIDE TO VIDEO PRODUCTION

There is a level of interpretation and meaning derived from well-composed visual representation. This chapter will provide you with a brief introduction to producing meaningful videos with excellence.

## PREPRODUCTION

• Figure out the audience.

Video producers, whether at the network, on the freelance beat, or operating a media ministry within the church, have clients. A client, even if a ministry representative, is the person with the message. The producer is the interpreter, assisting the client in translating the message into an effective visual form. Most of the time this does not mean copying the client's ideas to videotape verbatim, because these ideas may be misdirected, if they're not developed through proper questions put to the client. (The producer is a diplomat, who may be getting the client to agree that he or she has an ambiguous message.) Some of the questions include:

What is the message?
Again, be very clear about a specific message. And stick to it.

Who is the audience?

The worship venue dictates a different style for presentation than does a meeting, or a lecture in the classroom. The worship video may be celebratory, or it may be required to fit within established themes for a particular weekend. Although all video is persuasive, this is particularly true for large events. There is an inverse relationship between the size of the audience and their collective attention span.

How many people will see it?

Is the video clip to be distributed or consumed simultaneously by the audience? Some things will work better in a group setting. Stopping the video for reflection, for instance, wouldn't work in large groups, but it may be appropriate for small-group or individual viewing.

• Determine the hook.

Develop a hook, or a root metaphor, that makes the video compelling. The hook in literature is sometimes called the recurring motif, or the broad mechanism that conveys the theme for the story. This may be visual or aural. Read the preceding section on metaphor (pages 57–58) if you are struggling to name a hook for a video clip. Furthermore, every video has a dynamic element that moves the other pieces along, which helps the hook sink deeply into the viewer. The music bed often drives a videotaped montage, whereas stories are often driven more deeply by the interviewee's voice.

• Write it down and draw it out.

Sketch out your ideas as part of the creative process. Write a script or storyboard for visual ideas. It is always helpful to pen thoughts and ideas, and spend time in brainstorming sessions with creative people. Scripting is good for a developed plan (although invariably it changes depending on what the captured video footage produces). Storyboarding refers to actually drawing out in little boxes, which represent frames or screens, how you imagine the video to look. This is not necessary for some of what you want to do, but it will be helpful for more program-oriented pieces, or as preparation for specific camera takes in time-sensitive locations. For example, if given permission to shoot on government property for two hours, it would be wise to know ahead of time exactly how you'd like the images to look in a frame.

# PRODUCTION

- The A-roll, or the interview

Decide if interviews, or "talking heads," are needed. Pick people and schedule interviews. In some forms, video is testimony-driven. That is, personal stories compose the bulk of the narration. Thus, interviewing may often be the foundation of shooting video. In lieu of A-roll, voice-over tracks are common. *Voice-over* means narration without video of the person speaking. An example of this is reporter commentaries in news packages.

- The B-roll, or the environment

Decide on B-roll and a time to shoot it. It can be anything related to the topic, and is often the illustration of the matching voice-over. Lack of B-roll in video kills momentum. In production, there's an adage that you can never have enough B-roll. Shoot many more shots than you would ever need. You'll thank yourself in postproduction.

# POSTPRODUCTION

- Pick the right music.

At Ginghamsburg we reviewed the previous weekend services on Wednesdays. During one worship review meeting, I was chatting with a few teammates about the impact of a video from the previous weekend. We felt that the piece, a recruitment tool for the church's men's ministry, had been effective. Suddenly, the music person pointed out with pride, "Well, it's the music that makes it!"

Of course it was. Some of the best scenes in film history wouldn't have worked without a powerful score underneath. Scenes from *Rocky*, when Sylvester Stallone jogs to the top of the Philadelphia Museum of Art, or *Apocalypse Now*, when the squadron of helicopters attacks a Vietcong delta to the accompaniment of Wagner's "Ride of the Valkyries," were both dependent on the emotional impact of the musical score. As a designer of media, don't underestimate the power of audio in a video production.

But you must be discerning about musical selection. Watch TV commercials if you want to learn about the persuasive impact of music. One fun exercise is to try watching a few commercials without sound. You may find that the meaning of the commercials you see is dramatically different. Good video requires both effective shots and an emotional audio bed.

Remember that copyright applies, particularly for nonworship applications. That favorite song or jazz piece may not be legal to use. For guidance on copyright issues, see the Bonus Materials at www.thewiredchurch2.com.

It may be cost-effective to invest a few hundred dollars in CDs containing copyright-free music that is designed for video applications. These CDs may be purchased in one of five ways:

1. Needle-drop, the studio practice of keeping large libraries on hand and paying publishers per use (costs which are then passed on to clientele, similarly to how iStockphoto sells visual images). This tends to be, long-term, the most expensive route for churches.
2. Buyout, or the permanent purchase of single CDs or libraries from a publisher, which gives the user all rights for reuse. This works for light church use, where all the selections aren't heard in the first month.
3. Licensing, or a short-term buyout, usually purchased by the year. Most of the highest-quality libraries may be licensed. For heavy use, licensing may be the best church option, since a library can be squeezed dry and then returned to the publisher within a certain time frame.
4. Individual Download, where a user can pay a single fee on the Internet for a musical bed and its matching license.
5. Music Software, such as Adobe Audition or Apple Soundtrack, which provide instrumentation and the ability to compose your own score.

Music production companies may be found in trade magazines and over the Internet. Most will forward a demo or sample CDs for perusal prior to financial arrangements.

• Log your footage.

Logging is the process of dictating all the shots recorded on tape or disc, often with notations regarding width of shot, length, beginning time-code, quality, and a brief description. Logging becomes more necessary for the larger production, and it can be tedious. But it is a vital step in knowing what you have to work with to ensure the best production.

• Choose your best shots and discard the rest.

Be extremely selective. Sometimes it is necessary to go through the painful process of leaving great stuff on the "cutting room floor" if it doesn't belong with the central topic of the video. Stay focused.

• Edit your piece together.

Be sure to compose and integrate computer graphics. See graphics for further detail on design.

Allow one hour for every minute of straight video editing, and at least twice that for graphics-intensive video. If you don't have your own equipment, various postproduction houses in most communities have per-hour rates that include an operator. Many often provide off-hour times to nonprofit clientele as a write-off. Another option is to check into cable access studios, which are available in many larger cities and offer midrange-quality equipment for public use. See part 4 for types of video editing systems.

• Don't forget distribution.

How will people see it? If it is in worship, then set up TVs or projection equipment and make sure video plays back well and at good volume. If in homes, then make the appropriate number of copies, or post online as a Flash video.

## SUGGESTED VIDEO RESOURCES

• Video Production Handbook, by Gerald Millerson

A basic guide with practical tips from a master of television-station culture. (He also wrote a tome full of technical know-how entitled *The Technique of Video Production*. The first is the beginner's version of the second.)

• DV Magazine

An excellent, long-running periodical resource, now published online, for the level of production apropos to a local church ministry.

• Television

Watching TV at home critically, with attention to composition, shot sequence, edits, and graphic style, is one of the best ways to learn video. For training purposes, commercials are better than programming. Late-night talk shows and live performances are also laboratories for instruction on short-form (2-3 minute) video. Even features on star athletes before sporting events give stylistic examples of how to compose short-form stories.

• Somebody else's stuff

If you think of something you've seen that fits the bill as well as something you could create, check into purchasing a copy with usage rights. Be tenacious. You'd be surprised how often copyright holders will accommodate your needs. I put calls to a number of local PBS affiliates around the country in search of someone to sell me a Bill Nye episode that would help me on a call-to-worship video clip. When I found the person, she was more than happy to sell me a copy of the tape and granted permission to use it in worship.

Caveat: a request for nonprofit use often doesn't go over well at commercial networks. Networks will likely never grant you permission to use anything they broadcast because they fear illegal copying and reproduction of broadcast material and because broadcasters are tuned into the present use rather than the reuse of their footage. It is generally not worth the effort to approach them.

For more possibilities for preproduced video clips, see the list of Worship Media Resources in the Bonus Materials at www.thewiredchurch2.com.

CHAPTER 10

# HOW TO MAKE GREAT GRAPHICS

## GRAPHICS 101: COMPUTER TECHNOLOGY AND IMAGE MAKING

• Work with a primary image for the event.

Represent the metaphor visually through a single title or headline graphic that may be used periodically to reinforce the theme. The title graphic should state the theme either with imagery, text, or both.

• Give it the business. In other words, treat it.

Keep your graphics simple, bold, and fun to look at, but representative of television culture rather than computer culture. Television is our dominant cultural medium. Although a majority of homes have PCs, 99 percent have TVs, and over half are homes with multiple TV sets. In other words, imitate the dominant culture of TV, not the painful look of PowerPoint computer culture. Use the forms of broadcast television rather than PowerPoint-presentation pie charts. Use light and shadows (see below) to provide depth.

• Establish a style.

Pick a style and use it consistently for the duration of the event. Choose a consistent color scheme and typography. Use it for Scripture, sermon points, and graphic images. Make it present throughout the event in some fashion. This is called establishing an identity.

• Color

As documented by psychologists, color has an impact on perception and retention, and therefore its importance shouldn't be underestimated. Cool colors like blue, green, and purple have a calming effect, while warms like red, yellow, and orange are more stirring. In fact, red has been shown in studies to increase pulse and breathing rates, and blue to calm them. Many colors, in fact, have connotations with subliminal effects. Red may be associated with desire, passion, or violence. Green may evoke money or nature. When used together, red, white, and blue, of course, are good for patriotic days.

Further, for screen use, high contrast is important, usually light text on dark or deep backgrounds. Good color combination examples include yellow on blue, orange on purple, and white on almost anything dark.

Again, for instruction, watch TV, especially local and national news programs, which make heavy use of graphics with bright, complementary colors.

• Fonts

There are two basic types of fonts: display, or headline fonts, and copy, or body fonts. Display fonts are goofy and unusual fonts, and copy fonts are normal, often traditional, and never the twain should meet. It's not much fun to read Scripture on screen in Cookie Cutter or Dodge City font, although that might be appropriate for the reference or heading.

• Lead the eye

Western culture tracks movement left to right, top to bottom. This means that graphic elements need to be positioned and balanced accordingly. Don't put an image in the bottom right corner, facing to the right, as this will lead an eye out of the frame. For example, if the background image is a landscape with a mountain in the upper left corner, and a tree in the lower right corner, then text should be placed around the tree, middle and lower left, left-justified, maintaining balance with the background.

The rule of thirds is a grid that divides the frame into 9 parts, like a tic-tac-toe board, for the purpose of composing elements. Apply the rule of thirds to your graphics as a test for composition, and make sure that the elements are distributed accordingly, with the focal or main visual point preferably near an intersection of two of the lines in the grid.

• Space

Use a lot of space within and in between graphic elements. Elements are each of the objects in an image, whether they are display headlines, images of any size, or blocks of text. Avoid visual clutter. Leave plenty of space for elements to have their being, and space to insert additional elements and illustrations.

• Lines

Random elements may be brought together in a cohesive fashion through the use of lines and frames. For example, titles and points can rest on a semitranslucent bar. A common example is the recurring trend in design to use thick black borders to create boxes for images and information, or the use of multiple crossing lines to provide texture and direct attention toward the focal point.

• Crop images

Delete all the unnecessary data around a subject to focus the viewer's attention to the purpose of the image. This is particularly the case when using images for illustrations, such as a newspaper headline, or when picking one person from a crowd.

Also, don't crop people at their joints, for it is visually jarring. Leave headroom and space in front of profiled faces, to maintain continuity.

• Light and shadow

The primary technique that separates the amateur artist from the professional is the use of imaginary lights on the surface of the graphic, which creates corollary shadows. Light and shadows can give a solid color depth and direct the eye to the purpose of the image. They can turn a simple circle into a floating bubble or ball. Some programs have light-producing filters; blurring light and dark areas achieves similar results.

For a much more in-depth analysis of making images for worship, see *Design Matters: Creating Powerful Imagery for Worship* (Nashville: Abingdon Press, 2006).

# GRAPHICS 201: ADVANCED GRAPHICS TIPS

Here is a set of random tips for finding the subtle differences that separate the amateurs from the experts.

- How do I know when to represent a metaphor or sermon illustration with a graphic?

Always say the same thing, but in a different way. Realize that each medium has strengths and weaknesses, and that some things are best left to oral communication. Don't try to illustrate every word picture that a speaker offers, some of which are too minor or temporary to warrant imagery. Keep to primary points and illustrations.

- How picky should I be about the timing of a graphic that is displayed behind a speaker?

Studies have shown that there are direct relationships between the timing of graphics and voice-over narration, and their impact on viewer retention. One study examined graphics that are timed in seven-second intervals preceding and following voice-over narration, up to twenty-one seconds in each direction. The results showed that graphics synchronized with voice-over and graphics preceding the voice-over by seven seconds had a much higher retention rate for the viewer than those preceded by fourteen or twenty-one seconds or followed by seven, fourteen, or twenty-one seconds. The differences were as much as 30 percent in retention of the image for the viewer. So if the pressures of exactly matching an errant preacher's ramblings are too intense, err on the early side.

- Should I add text in an image manipulation program, such as Adobe PhotoShop, or in presentation software, such as Microsoft Power-Point?

There are advantages each way, depending on the particular software application. Most presentation programs are incapable of doing more advanced effects such as blurred drop shadow or glow, both of which are features of graphics from TV culture and not computer culture. These must be accomplished in an image manipulation program. But designs created in such programs are more difficult to edit in case of error. As a rule of thumb, only do main points, or the display font graphics, in image programs, as these are less likely to be edited. Then produce body copy such as Scriptures and song lyrics in presentation programs, which are easily changeable.

- I can't take photographs, and I draw like my four-year-old. Is there any hope?

Fortunately for you, entrepreneurial artists had you in mind when they created resource libraries of images and art. These libraries consist of everything you'd want, from textured backgrounds to clip art and photo galleries. Most are relatively cheap, too. The Internet is a great place to find them. For a list, see the section Worship Media Resources in the Bonus Materials at www.thewiredchurch2.com.

PART THREE

# BUILDING A CHAMPIONSHIP CREW

CHAPTER 11

# ESTABLISH THE GAME PLAN

Don't do media ministry alone. Don't even try. On a vacation to the Florida Keys, I visited the home of Ernest Hemingway, which since his death has been turned into a museum. Part of the tour led me by his writing studio, a loft apartment with walls of books, two or three chairs, and a single desk. The tour guide said that while in Florida, Hemingway did all of his writing in this room. It was a quiet, isolated room, obviously meant for one person, alone with his thoughts.

Compare that to the studios I encountered while an intern at CBS Television City in Hollywood. One night while there I witnessed a live production of *The Late Late Show* with Tom Snyder, which aired following *The Late Show with David Letterman*, at 12:30 a.m. EST. Eight people sat in one small room, many talking simultaneously, limbs and chairs bumping. These "authors" were practically sitting on top of one another! This creative environment was not a space for Hemingway, to be sure. However, each person in the crew served a particular purpose and was critical to the success of the production, which was being watched by literally millions of people across the continent. The same was true for many other productions that I witnessed, including sitcoms, original television events, and feature films.

Team-oriented production is central to digital media. Although ministry in the age of the printed word was largely individual, ministry in the digital age is like a television studio, operating with a number of specialists who accomplish more than would be possible by a single author, no matter how gifted. Digital media authors are now able to create more with less than mass print authors because of the coordinated efforts of teams. Developing effective teams for both the creation and presentation of digital media in local church environments will be the key to success for media in ministry.

# THE IMPORTANCE OF UNPAID TEAM MEMBERS

The crew of unpaid people is at the heart of an effective ministry. Ministry for the digital culture is not about what staff to hire to accomplish the tasks at hand. It is about empowering laypersons to utilize their gifts in ways they never thought possible for the purpose of advancing God's kingdom. You will discover that as the media ministry develops, it becomes an entry point for people previously not part of the church community. Because of the opportunity to use their gifts and talents, individuals may even join the team and become regular attendees at the church. Like the movie *Field of Dreams*, once you build it, people will come. Remember, in our postliterate world, production skills are no longer confined to the trained and highly experienced few. Now, it seems that everyone posts to YouTube and Flickr. People have commented that through media and art, they are discovering opportunities to use their gifts in service to God's kingdom in ways they previously had not thought possible.

Once I asked a film student at a local state college to create a two-minute promotional piece to recruit people to sound ministry. The student, Dave, got three friends from campus to help him make the spot. None were a part of our church community, but following production of the spot, two of the three became regular attendees!

The temptation—once you have discovered talented, committed people—is to pay them to ensure that your team will not collapse on some given weekend. But relationships get a bit complicated when a team becomes a mix of paid and unpaid people, for a number of reasons.

The addition of money, especially with Christians who are young in their faith, can obscure motives for services given and interfere with their growth in giving as an expression of faith. As pastor Wayne Cordeiro states, the act of serving is not so much about what the servant is doing but rather who they are becoming.[1] Paid persons have a tendency to hoard knowledge as a form of job security. Paying servants can also lead to the game of secret keeping—does director number one, who is paid to direct, know that director number two is not paid? If so, then does director number one suddenly begin having an inflated sense of importance regarding his or her work in the ministry? Or if not, then does director number one make the mistake of telling director number two about the payment? Such knowledge would obviously hurt efforts in building community. Further, paid staff is no hedge against missed deadlines or failed projects. Unpaid volunteers usually have different, and sometimes more altruistic, motives.

One of the two young film students who came to our congregation during the production of the spot was given the opportunity to become part-time staff to handle the increase in demand for media in education. Although he was an excellent unpaid team member, the expectations and pressure of being paid staff were too much at that stage of his professional and faith development. After a year in that capacity we removed him from a job that did not fit him. He returned to his unpaid role and excelled as a director with strong technical skills. Now, ten years later, he is in full-time media ministry.

For the first two and a half years of media ministry at Ginghamsburg Church, as weekly worship attendance tripled in size from one thousand to three thousand, I was the only paid media staff person among an unpaid team of ninety people. Through that team we accomplished great things and set the stage for the mix of paid and unpaid team members that was to follow. It is through unpaid people, pursuing their gifts and talents in ways they never dreamed possible, that a media ministry can transform lives and build the Kingdom.

## ESTABLISH GOALS FOR YOUR TEAMS

For what purpose will your teams be working? Do you wish to coordinate digital media into the worship context, or education, or both? Will the media you create be a part of your community experience once a month? Every week? These questions must be answered before you can begin. Brainstorm with your colleagues about your goals for media use. For ideas, see chapter 8 for a list of the ways to use media.

Goal-setting in media ministry can quickly go to an expensive place. The challenge of media professionals in church life is to act out of what you have, not out of what you don't have. Regardless of the quality of the media equipment available at your disposal, it probably will not compare to what a professional studio has. But take heart! The tools for making digital culture have become democratized. The landscape for media continues to change drastically as home systems become increasingly powerful.

One of the first famous viral videos on the Internet was a satire called *Troops* (a ten-minute hybrid of *Star Wars* and the TV show *Cops*). It was produced by a twenty-something in California with a home system, and it was so effective it received national attention and the feedback of *Star Wars* creator George Lucas. I downloaded it from the Internet when it came out. The quality of the short film is amazing. The lesson: do not underestimate the creative power of media creation for local church environments, regardless of supposed technological limitations.

The challenge for novices, on the other hand, is not to bite off more than one can chew. Remember that mediocre media is worse than none at all, because it doesn't communicate. Mediocre media distracts. So do what you can, and do it well. Your creativity, and that of your team, will be such that you want to try great things. Risk-taking is part of the makeup of any media guru, and the only way to grow, but always pass those risks through the test of excellence. It's a difficult balance to maintain.

# CREATE A CULTURE OF *KOINONIA*

*Koinonia: the harmonious fellowship of believers who share a common mission.* *Koinonia* is a New Testament word that is variously translated as "fellowship," "sharing," or "partnership." It's the experience of harmony through Christ that can happen when a community of Christians works together for a common goal. You don't have to make it happen as a leader, either; it is a gift from the Holy Spirit. Your function is to provide the freedom for the expression of this gift, and to encourage team members' passion when the gift is apparent. One way to energize the team is to constantly cast stories of transformation in the lives of people who attend the church.

Digital media plays a role in individual transformation as well. Once at Ginghamsburg Church I produced a worship segment telling the testimony of a young couple coming to faith. The video story, like no other medium, described a couple heartbroken at the loss of their newborn baby, but held up through the love and support of the church community. A few months after that worship experience, I witnessed how media elements not only used their story to inspire others, but actually inspired the couple as well. At a later worship service, we closed with video and audio of ultrasound from an unborn baby being carried by the preacher's wife. The sight and sound of that unborn baby on the big screen were a cathartic experience for the grieving couple. Of course, emotions are complex, and the opposite could have happened—they could have been overwhelmed with pain and jealousy. The point is, however, that media resonates, and elicits reactions in viewers. Media is not the communication form of a stagnant church. It will cause change and growth. It will jerk your congregation out of their apathy and indifference.

As your church grows, relay stories of life-changing work to the team, and make sure they understand their role in transforming the community.

# QUALITIES TO LOOK FOR

## People Who Catch Your Vision

More important than technical mastery is the condition of the person's spirit. Sometimes a little technical expertise without an understanding of the vision of the ministry can be dangerous, particularly when you are forced to rely on individuals with a greater degree of technical knowledge than you have.

It is very important in a team environment to have technical accountability. Don't just let the people loose, because ultimately they are not responsible for the care and use of the equipment. There's nothing worse than a carefully planned and produced service ruined by an over-tweaked projector or soundboard. (See the Bonus Materials section at www.thewiredchurch2.com for a pre-worship checklist on confirming all the details!)

## Soft Skills and Hard Skills

It is just as important to have people-oriented leaders and administrators in ministry as it is to have technically apt people. I specifically recruit non-technical people and train them because it is easier to teach video skills than it is to teach people skills.

In *Doing Church as a Team*, Wayne Cordeiro says that when you're starting a ministry, your first step is to recruit four leaders.[2] Cordeiro argues, and my experience supports, that a leader will have difficulty discipling more than four people at once. A small group of five (four plus the leader) can easily stay focused on the joint mission and, more importantly, won't burn out. Keep those four leaders within your care, no less and no more, for the duration of the ministry, regardless if the community is ten or three hundred people. These four people will be the heart of the ministry and will raise a team strong in number and spirit beyond what you could accomplish single-handedly. In Cordeiro's design, your four leaders, before they actually begin *doing* the work of ministry, turn around and find four other people in their area of expertise.

These leaders don't necessarily have to fit the ministry's needs by function or role. The job of the ministry director—you—is to take their mix of gifts and apply them in whatever way best fits the team, just as a coach adapts his team's strategy based upon the strengths of the team's players. As to who these four people shall be, they are the four who exhibit the most passion for the ministry and have the best ability to articulate their passion and lead others.

Say for example you have someone who loves graphic design. They might become one of your four people. But before they start producing graphics, they in turn find four other people with whom to work, dividing responsibilities. Maybe one person handles worship images, another handles looping announcement images, another website images, and the fourth print communication images. These four people might even find four more for each responsibility, and further divide the task. You can go as "deep" as you want.

## Technical Proficiency

Every church has introverts with great computer and video skills. This ministry is made for them. Although not necessarily your leaders, they are the ones who will be able to step in immediately with the skills necessary to get the ministry running. Many people are visual learners (hence the need for media ministry!), and will only see the power of media in communicating the gospel by seeing it in action. When these techno-geniuses put on the initial worship experiences, possibilities will become evident and others will come. They can then become your trainers as you bring in other people to grow the team.

# CHAPTER 12
# THE ROSTER OF A WINNING MEDIA MINISTRY

Media ministry may be organized into any number of volunteer teams, depending on church size. Teams may be creative or technical in nature. It is our experience that it is unusual to find volunteers who are both creatively and technically gifted. We recommend creating separate teams for each function. You could call them your left-brained and right-brained teams.

## CREATIVE TEAMS

Creative teams dream up worship services and media elements that communicate the power of the gospel through digital media. They may coordinate or even meet with other staff and volunteers in the church, such as music ministers and preachers, for the purpose of designing the entire worship service.

Note: They may or may not handle every aspect of the production, but they must understand what is entailed. It does no one any good for a "committee" to dream up time-lapse shots in a busy subway for a small church in a cornfield.

The makeup and process of leading a creative team is an entire subject in of itself, and is the subject of our forthcoming book, *Taking Flight with*

*Creativity: Worship Design Teams That Work* (Len Wilson and Jason Moore, Nashville: Abingdon Press, 2009).

# TECHNICAL TEAMS

## Team Organization

The technical team usually falls under the domain of the media minister. A well-organized approach to the live worship production is a must. One possibility is to create three subteams: video, sound/lighting, and duplication. The first two subteams function between worship and education. A typical production might require a crew of about ten: six video, two sound, one lighting, and one duplication. The ministry would then be structured on a weekly basis, with different crews serving a particular weekend of the month, all weekend. Schedules are established, with as little variation as possible, to ensure that each crew member always knows the particular time and date he or she is to serve. All team members serve the entire weekend, including Saturday rehearsal and worship if necessary, and Sunday worship.

The other obvious organization for the crew is to structure them by service time. For example, a congregation with three services on Sunday morning might have the 8:30 crew, the 9:45 crew, and the 11:00 crew. My experience has been that this is a more difficult way to organize the team. Having one crew for an entire weekend prevents constant rotation of positions, which can limit crew members' familiarity with the production, and thus inhibit the production's quality. Although team members are caught up in the details of production, making it difficult to actually worship the weekend that they serve, their commitment is for that weekend only, leaving them free to worship without distraction the other three weekends of the month.

The schedule remains fixed, ideally, but there is naturally a small rate of turnover, as media can develop into a large volunteer ministry. So there is a continual need for team members. Conduct training workshops periodically, alternating between team functions.

## Area of Expertise

Have each media ministry member choose an initial area of expertise. This self-selection does not encourage exclusivity; rather, a method of specialization enables everyone to serve in specific, needed ways. Media ministry is not like writing a book; it requires the skills and talents of several gifted people working in cooperation for the good of the whole.

Although the area of expertise is that which requires your team members' primary attention, have them be aware of processes in every area, as knowledge is cumulative and creates a better working team environment. For example, the computer operator should have at least a rudimentary understanding of how to mix live video. Empathy and understanding are crucial to an effective ministry; a functioning knowledge of the entire media ministry enables this to happen. The best leaders are the ones who have experience at every level of operation. Team leaders are much less likely to call for the impossible or create tension out of ignorance if they understand the demands on the other team members.

## Committing to Serve

Encourage team members to realize their commitment to serve in the media ministry, before they decide to join because it is "cool." Digital media is intrinsic to worship, and team members are a vital part of the process. When a new visitor walks in, one of the first and most lasting impressions will be what is displayed on the big screen of the wired church. Our task in media ministry is to create and present excellent digital media to communicate the message of the transforming power and love of Jesus Christ. We want that first impression to be a good one, and subsequent experiences to be of effective communication with minimal mess-ups. Thus, their trustworthy participation is necessary, and the media ministry could not function completely without each member's presence and dedication to ministry tasks. Part of that commitment means abiding by certain norms, which are suggested as follows:

- You are expected to serve when scheduled. If you cannot serve, then you are expected to inform your team leader at least twenty-four hours in advance. We understand that there are times when you will not be able to serve when you are scheduled, but please make an attempt to give the team leader as much notice as possible. In lieu of a team leader, contact the coordinating staff person.
- The people of the media ministry are a voice of encouragement. Never, in the intensity of live production, let your commitment to excellence outweigh your love for one another.

- Correction is to be done in a loving and caring way. We can fix any-thing that goes wrong with the equipment, procedures, and processes we use in media ministry. Repairing a broken heart can take a long time.
- You are expected to follow the rules of the ministry.
- You are expected to work the assignments or tasks you accept.
- You are expected to serve at least one weekend per month.
- You are expected to attend three worship services per month; a steady diet of worship is important to your spiritual growth, and also to your understanding of the rapidly developing area of media in worship.

## Team Roles

My "top seven" list of important media functions, in alphabetical order:
- Camera operator: Activities include live production, under the direc-tor's lead, and field production for preproduced clips.
- Computer operator: Creates or operates computer system(s) to project images, video, and animations—which includes text for praise and wor-ship songs, and hopefully much more—onto the screen during live events.
- Director: Works with all team members (including audio and lighting) and the speaker. The director is the leader of the crew and gives the commands to other operators on the headset system.
- Duplication: Records live events; makes copies to disc and/or cassette tape of these for sale and distribution.
- Lighting: Programs and operates the lighting board for live events.
- Sound: Operates live sound events, including setup, gain, equalization, and mixing.
- Technical director: Operates the digital device through which the vari-ous sources of video are mixed for projection.

# TEAM-BUILDING TIPS AND TECHNIQUES

## Build Depth

The introduction of a media ministry in church life, particularly in worship, is one of the more demanding challenges among all the possi-bilities emerging in digital media culture. As we say at seminars, even tel-evision sitcoms take a thirteen-week break every summer, but worship occurs fifty-two Sundays a year! The best way to avoid burnout is to build depth within the team. As a coach, spend a percentage of your time each week building teams, even if this cuts into your personal production schedule. A personal rule of thumb is to try to spend on average ten hours per week in relationship-building and training. A team with depth can better handle the transitions of life and continue to move ahead in ministry. The alternative is a small remnant who are asked to carry the whole ministry forward and ammunition for naysayers who resist change and growth.

Media ministry is a complex hybrid of existing styles of digital and electronic communication. It is not broadcast television, certainly; it is not PowerPoint for the office; and it is not home videos of the backyard cookout. Its purpose is not to entertain. As a new, interpretive communication tool, it requires adaptability through which unskilled people do not have to unlearn anything. They're moldable, without preconceived notions.

Although it's pleasant to have professionals at your disposal, don't be jealous of the large church in Southern California with many professional volunteers, or despair at the perceived lack of talent. Often the most committed, highly trained team members are the ones with little previous experience, beyond a desire to learn about and serve others through a media ministry.

## Cross-train

Move your team members, with their consent, every six to twelve months. Many people will get bored in a single capacity and might leave the media ministry. Training them in multiple functions, or cross-training them, makes team breadth and depth greater. Don't rely on any one person too much.

## Rehearsals

As you begin to put together technical crews, conduct a series of technical rehearsals prior to "opening day," with a few people to witness the event. Over time, as your team develops, continue to use the rehearsal time as an opportunity to get some hands-on time for your newer members.

## Develop a Farm System

Look for media venues outside of worship, such as youth and education functions, where the number of people gathered at any one time is fewer. These events become a farm system, a means of training and tracking the potential of future skilled players. Smaller functions provide an ideal hands-on training environment, while not sacrificing the quality of the primary event.

Even the youth themselves can become a farm team of sorts as you identify and cultivate young talent. One church trusted God's desire for people's gifts to be used for the purpose of the Kingdom and mobilized a group of junior high youth to create video for inside and outside their church community. The children called themselves VidKidz. Given freedom, the kids are doing incredible things with the internal church communications and community outreach. Their efforts include a mission awareness project in which VidKidz used cable access equipment to do a series of "On the Street" interviews during the local community's annual March for Jesus rally. Pastor Ken Dewalt says that the biggest part of the story is that at the time, their church was a recent startup, with an average attendance of fifty-eight. He says,

> We often get the question, "How can such a small church support so many small groups and cool stuff like VidKidz?" Any church that decides to be a permission-giving church can do it. Letting go, and letting God, never meant more to me than it does after serving here for a year and a half. And someday we'll be able to move from overheads to PowerPoint in worship because we asked our kids to take over the mixing boards and the video cameras!

There are groups of people in your church, many young, itching for the opportunity to use their creativity and gifts in design and production for something meaningful. Because media literacy, or as Leonard Sweet calls it, "graphicacy," is innate in younger generations, God will provide the creative and the technical means to accomplish the mission that God has set forth.

# CHAPTER 13

# TRAINING CAMP FOR YOUR TEAM

## VIDEOGRAPHERS

The camera operator is the foundation of any video team. The camera eye is the most often seen, visible ministry function of most media-equipped churches. When visitors enter the church for the first time in multisensory worship, the cameras are often one of the primary elements that they notice. And an effective use of cameras may play an important role in the return visit of an unchurched person.

At a basic level, the camera in worship serves as a viewing aid to those who sit some distance away from the platform. It brings immediacy to events and to the spoken word by bringing the action to the congregation. For example, a baptism may be obscured to many in the congregation, but a camera close-up can capture the moving moment for everyone to experience. Preachers may discover their effectiveness increases when people can not only hear their voice clearly but see their facial expressions as well. Additionally, when well composed and ordered, the camera brings meaning to the elements of a live event. It is thrilling to watch a carefully directed, intentionally chosen camera sequence during a live musical piece.

Camera operators must be smooth and steady. They must have a good eye for composing a shot because the director doesn't have time to talk them through shot composition during the intensity of a production. They must remain calm, stay focused on the subject or object they are shooting, be prepared to accept last-second changes, and smoothly execute transitions.

## The Art of Good Camerawork

Each shot should make a point. The composition of a slot directly impacts the effectiveness of the larger production. Here are three bad scenarios to avoid:

- Too much in the shot distracts; the viewer's eye is distracted and flits around but concentrates on nothing.
- Too little in the shot loses the viewer's attention.
- Worst of all, when there are no visual accents to grab the attention, the eye may wander.

With proper arrangement of elements so that the main subject stands out from the surroundings, audiences will remain focused on the subject. A well-balanced shot will have a settled, stable feel to it. The frame position of a subject can affect whether the picture looks balanced or lopsided.

## Anticipation

A good camera operator successfully anticipates the action, whether from the floor or from directors' commands. If the subject of a shot steps out of frame, a good operator will smoothly follow to regain the shot. For worship, this may occur anytime, for example, when a speaker bends down or suddenly steps to one side or another. If such an event happens, do not wait for the director's command (which will possibly be "FOLLOW—NOW!"), but smoothly adjust the camera to regain the frame. A good camera operator will set up shots on his or her own initiative. During music performance, for example, operators may quickly set up shots for the director's choosing when their camera is not the one being projected.

## Framing

Most monitors and screens are adjusted to get the maximum picture size possible; however, all cut off at least a small portion of the outer edge of a shot, usually 4-5 percent. Most projectors, however, display the entire image. What the lens perceives is what the projector displays. So be careful! Compose the shot to keep the important details within the "safe area" of the screen. The safe area is the guaranteed portion that will show in a television or monitor, and is marked by a white box in many camera viewfinders. If there's no box in your little camera window, just imagine one, about 10 percent in from the outer edge, and don't put important material too close to the edges.

What's the best way to frame an image? The rule of thirds is an easy guide for placing subjects in the frame. Draw or imagine a "tic-tac-toe" grid on the frame. Simply compose subjects so that their weight is distributed along the lines that you created, or where the lines cross. Things to avoid:

• A horizon located halfway up the frame, as it is boring.
• A head in the very center of the frame.

Example: A close-up shot of a "talking head" should be composed so that their eyes are on the top horizontal line (called the "golden line" in industry parlance). This is because the eyes communicate more than any other facial feature. Such a shot puts the top of the subject's head above the line and the rest of their face or body below. It uses enough of the screen without the atmosphere crushing down on the person. When positioned on the left or right third (with their nose on a vertical line), this is known as the "four-hanky" interview, which is useful for testimony clips!

It is often tempting to devise shots that are different (e.g., from a distorted perspective or using reflections or low angles). These shots are fine when created for a dramatic effect. But in many situations, unusual viewpoints don't merely make the picture look different; they draw attention to the technique and distract us from the subject. To break the rule of thirds, you've got to know it and have a substantial purpose for your decision.

When framing shots, work with what you have. Don't ignore some of the elements in a frame to center on one or two. If it's in the shot, use it in framing the shot (e.g., your subject may be framed well, with a left center close-up, but the composition would be ruined if in doing so you ignore the instrumentalist behind him or her, halfway off the edge of the frame).

Make sure to leave "headroom." Keep a check on the distance between the top of a person's head and the top of the frame. If the headroom is too little, the frame will appear to crush a person and part of someone's head may be cut off. If the headroom is too much, it puts the shot out of balance, which will distract the audience. Check with your presenters; they may not appreciate the perception of a squashed bug on the screen.

## Balance

Balance plays an important role with multiple objects in a frame.

Grab your camera and try the following: First, position a large object on one side of the screen with several smaller objects on the other side. How do you compose the frame so that the eye is drawn to a specific object and the other objects don't interfere? Balance is a matter of relative size and distance from the center of the frame. Second, try framing the same subject from a different angle. If there are a number of separate items in a picture, they will look better when they are grouped in some way, rather than scattered around the frame. You can create the effect of unity in the picture, even when the subjects are some distance apart, by carefully selecting the direction from which you shoot them.

It is possible to vary the relative proportions and positions of elements in a frame by:

- Adjusting the camera distance; the closer they are, the larger they appear.
- Changing the camera height; the lower the camera, the more prominent the objects in the foreground become.
- Changing the camera lens angle; using a wide-angle lens makes things rapidly diminish in size with distance.

Try composing a frame in which one object is very close and another is far off. Notice the disparate effect caused by such great depth. This is a popular technique for television news videographers.

## Perpetual Motion: Left to Right

Remember that scene in *The Empire Strikes Back*, when Darth Vader is battling Luke Skywalker? Out by the bottomless donut-hole-thing, where Darth Vader chops off Luke's hand, Luke finds himself trapped. He is portrayed crouching in the lower right of the frame, with Darth Vader in the upper left.

Why are they positioned like that in the frame? Did George Lucas even think about that part? He sure did, and they are positioned like that because, as in many films, iconic shots are framed so that the hero is placed on the right side of the frame, and the villain on the left. (As Westerners, we read left to right, and we like to end on the hero.) Darth Vader, villain, was defeating Luke Skywalker, hero, so he stood taller in the frame. Being positioned higher up evokes power and superiority.

Our eyes are trained to read left to right. Engaging movement, then, is left to right in a frame. When you want to portray triumph, try panning lower left to upper right, rising up to meet the hero!

## Perpetual Motion: Leading

Always allow room for objects to move within a frame. For example, if a speaker is profiled in a frame, position him or her on the side opposite the direction they are pointing. This gives them room to move. It may be helpful to think of the speaker needing room to fill up a big talking balloon with all those thoughts.

Ditto for when he or she is moving. Give subjects leading room to move within the frame so they don't appear about to jump off the edge of the frame.

## Perpetual Motion: Shooting the Action

Camera operators should be cognizant of the context of their shooting environment. What is the point of the production, and who is being featured? Always focus on the action in the environment. If it's the singer, focus on the singer; ditto for the guitar solo. When in multi-camera environments, there is usually a camera designated by the director as the primary camera. If the opportunity arises in this context, look for quick cutaways to other elements in the environment. See the director section (pages 105–10) for details on shot selection.

One more tip: If you make a mistake, act profound. Viewers may think that you are creating a new convention.

# PREPARATION FOR WORSHIP

Here is a checklist for camera operators preparing for worship and other live events:

- If using manned camera stations, set up all cameras into the switcher. If using remote systems, flip the "on" switch.

- Confirm the existence of a functioning signal path. In other words, turn on the camera and see the image on the projector. If no image exists, begin replacing elements in the signal path, such as individual cables, one at a time until you discover the source of the problem. Keep notes as problems arise so that you can develop a troubleshooting checklist, and keep the list in a visible space where the entire team has access to it.

## COMPUTER OPERATORS

The computer operator is responsible for the creation and or display of all graphics for worship and other live ministry productions. Graphic design and production are covered in part 2 and in *Design Matters: Creating Powerful Imagery for Worship* by Jason Moore and Len Wilson (Nashville: Abingdon Press, 2006).

## SWITCHERS/TECHNICAL DIRECTORS

The role of technical director, often called switcher or TD, is crucial because this person is the last stop before an image hits the big screen. The primary requirement for this position is a cool head. The TD must be able to operate the video mixer, without hesitation, in order to execute commands correctly and on time. On occasion, believe it or not, the director will lose focus or fall behind the pace of the production. The TD is the vice president, responsible for swearing himself or herself in and assuming command when necessary. And in the horrible case that something goes wrong on the screen, it is the finger of the TD that must hit the mixer, and quick!

Here are some important roles for a switcher:

- The switcher works closely with the director during production, functioning as his or her fingers.
- In addition to executing the choices for source input to the projector, the TD also keeps tabs on the quality of video coming from cameras, to assist the camera operators and the director if something is incorrect.
- The TD should have an accurate understanding of the video signal schematic (in other words, know which cable connects to what deck).

As it is the last stop before the big screen, the technical director also acts as a gatekeeper for what is projected. The gatekeeper is the decision-maker for the limited number of messages that may be transmitted through a given medium. If for some reason the director is not aware of a quality problem, the technical director can add value by monitoring output for quality control.

Contrary to what some may assume, the TD is more than simply a button pusher.

## The Switcher's Tools

There are a number of specific technical pieces that a switcher may need to know, including the video mixer, routers, scan doublers, and projectors. The first obvious device is for mixing all the video sources together before heading to the projector.

Many church-level **mixers** are designed for no more than four input sources. When a facility outgrows these four sources, it is necessary to add **routers**, which expand the number of possible inputs.

If you stare close enough at the TV, as your kids probably do, you will notice that the image, instead of being solid, is made up of a number of individual lines. A **scalar** or **scan doubler** controls the quality of the image on the screen by doing exactly as it proclaims: doubling the number of lines of video, or creating the illusion of high-definition television (HDTV). When television was originally invented, it was designed as a moving system of interlaced horizontal lines. In historical NTSC (North American Standards Committee) video, which is now also called standard definition, signals are limited to 525 horizontal lines of resolution. (Interlacing means that the lines are drawn on the screen in opposite intervals: odds, then evens. Standard television is interlaced, whereas RGB , or Red-Green-Blue, computer displays are noninterlaced, or progressive.)

Whereas 525 lines is plenty for small television monitors, images projected onto large surfaces often reveal these individual lines. (The original TV inventors never saw a need for televisions to be bigger than nineteen inches!) The scan doubler literally doubles these lines, projecting 1,050 lines of resolution to the big screen. In addition to enhancing resolution, the scan doubler has controls for other quality adjustments such as color, hue, brightness, and sharpness. In general, do not be rash about adjusting the projector: in equipped systems, it may be easier to tweak the doubler than the projector.

Around for more than twenty years now, the "high-definition" question continues to hang out just beyond reach for many producers and most local church media departments. As high-definition television gradually becomes more mainstream, and broadcasters switch their signals to HD, churches will eventually have to equip or convert their systems to be able to not just simulate the presence of more than 525 lines, but actually project more lines. The two standards for HD are 1080, either progressive or interlaced, or 720 progressive. This means that every piece of the system—from cameras, to computers, to switchers, to scalars, to projectors—will need to maintain the higher-quality signal. (This is partly why it's taking so long to implement!)

## Techniques of Switching

### Dissolves

Always look for an opportunity to avoid a sudden cut to an image during worship. Sudden movements when projected to a screen that is twenty feet tall can be abruptly disconcerting to worshipers. Most video mixers have mix options to allow a smooth transition between images. If you are operating without a mixer, try using black as a transition between various images.

### Fades

Another often used mixing feature is the fade. Though the goal of digital media in worship is to keep the visual language "spoken" at all times, there may occasionally be a need to go to black. Common instances include brief transitions between elements of worship or while a speaker is praying. Or, in covering mistakes! If the wrong image is projected, it is sometimes best to fade to black instead of showing several images while trying to get the right one on screen.

### Subtle Stuff

The TD can help create a mood during live events by varying the transition times and using the auto take and auto fade buttons rather than performing these functions manually. For example, standard worship dissolves may be fifteen frames (half a second), whereas prayer dissolves or fade to black at the end of a message might be forty-five frames. These nuances will come naturally with experience, and distinguish a more experienced TD operator. The TD can also assist the director and create a smoother, less intrusive flow for the images being projected. For example, in the course of a sermon, when the director gives the command to select a different source (e.g., "Take three"), the TD should wait until the end of a sentence. Try not to switch from one camera shot to another, or from computer back to camera in the middle of a sentence, or when there is an inordinate amount of movement in the cameras.

# CREW LEADERS/DIRECTORS

The director is the decision maker for what happens on the screen during worship, and is the glue for any live media event. Some of the basic functions of the director role include:

- Gives commands to all other team members.
- Tells the technical director which source to project, based on the given scripts.
- Interacts with the "stage" or "floor" director, who provides the congregational perspective and information about platform movement.
- Coaches the camera operators on establishing well-composed shots.
- Cues video and unique elements for projection, and calls them at the appropriate time (with some teams, it may make sense to allocate this function to someone else).

Because the director is the leader for the media team, it is important that he or she has at least a working knowledge of each of the pieces involved. Each role and each piece of equipment has idiosyncrasies. An effective director will know what to ask, and what not to ask, depending on the capabilities of the equipment.

## Anticipation

A good director anticipates like a chess player. The director must think ahead to the next few elements in the worship experience and communicate what is coming next to the team members. Time during transitions is critical during worship. An unprepared team that does not react quickly enough creates the pitfall of the "self-aware" moment, when worshipers leave the state of worship and become aware of the technical process. These moments of self-awareness precipitate the production complaint that Christian worship using digital media is merely entertainment.

Crisp, smooth navigation during the in-between moments of worship is key to the flow of a worship celebration. The congregation becomes unaware of the "production" behind the experience, just as the hearer of a powerful, moving sermon is unaware of the pauses and transitions in the preacher's voice. When the job is done right, all the attention is directed toward the experience of the "God-moment."

## Multitasking

The director must be capable of multitasking, which means managing multiple strains of thought simultaneously. Multitasking is a mainstreamed computer industry term for doing multiple things at the same time. The pace of our accelerated culture is such that the average person in our culture attempts multiple things simultaneously on a micro level, such as talking on the phone, writing a memo, and dealing with the person standing in the office. Even as the micro tasks are stacked, the same person is pursuing multiple agendas on a macro level, such as holding down a full-time job, attending school full-time, and starting a family. Most campus organizations have seen a dramatic decline in extracurricular attendance and participation because, unlike even ten years ago, most college students now attempt to hold down at least a twenty-hour-per-week job while going to school full time.

Multitasking is a part of the digital culture, and a good director should master this nonlinear system of thought or organization. During worship this means being cognizant of, literally, the Big Picture. What is happening at any given moment on the screen? The visual image is processed at a much quicker rate than is silent reading, or even listening. That means for worship there is never a dull moment. At each instant the screen must contain a relevant image, lest the viewer become distracted. Without even seeing a monitor, a preacher will know about a bad cue because the lack of recognition is evident in the faces of the congregation.

Perceiving the big picture, then, means viewing the succession of images on the screen through the eyes of the worshiper. For media ministers raised in a literate, linear society, this is not easy to do, particularly during moments when the pace of images is quick, such as while directing a song or when incorporating graphics and video into a sermon. It is easy, as a reaction to the pressure of the live event, to forget for a moment what is happening on the screen. The results can be damaging. I have stories of moments in worship when the camera operator loses focus and we get a shot of a person's feet. In panic, the director spends far too long trying to figure out an alternative, and the shot stays on the screen long enough to ruin whatever momentum the speaker had built. The pace of this culture is instant. Call the shot first, before you have time to think about it. Effectiveness can sometimes be about trusting your instincts as a leader.

## Keeping Your Cool

As goes the leader, so go the crew. The director must be able to respond to the unexpected with grace. Sometimes the speaker will forget or intentionally decide to skip a point or illustration, or give the improper cue. In that event, the director must reorganize and respond to the changes appropriately. For example, a director must decide on the spot if it is better to skip a graphic or bring it in late. Which will communicate the message to the congregation more clearly? Each service is different; with training and experience the right decisions will come.

## Techniques of Directing

### Single versus Multi-camera Shoots

Video production approaches include single camera environments and multi-camera environments.

Multi-camera production is usually live, using different viewing angles to document the event as it happens. Single-camera production, on the other hand, records all images to tape or disc, which are then edited together to form a final product. (Production is the process of recording images; postproduction is the compilation and arrangement of the images to form a final product.)

For example, a live NFL football game is a high-end, multi-camera production; the feature on the star athlete that precedes the event is often a single-camera segment produced prior to the broadcast. You might use multiple cameras for worship, a live environment, but a single camera for the produced video clips that are a part of worship.

Using more than one camera allows producers to capture the action from different angles and select certain shots through a switching device. It is important to alternate camera shots at appropriate moments. For example, do not switch to a camera shot when the speaker's back is toward that camera. It is better to stay with the selected shot until the speaker turns around, or choose another available option. In a multi-camera environment, team communication is the key—everyone must be able to hear the director.

### Shot Selection

Have you ever watched a spectacular live event on television? Most of the world watches one every year: the Super Bowl. In the dramatic closing moments of a live sporting event such as this, viewers expect to be pointed in the direction of the action, and are liable to get upset when shown a shot of a kid in the bleachers, exactly as the fourth-down pass is thrown.

The director is responsible for this shot selection. In order to keep attention in worship on the event, rather than on the people producing it, the director makes every shot intentional. This means a constant toggling between the focus of the moment and other, supporting elements. These secondary shots are called cutaways.

A common example of the need for effective shot selection occurs in featured numbers during worship, which might be sung by the choir. An appropriate shot selection in such a case might be:

• Opening medium shot of band
• Medium shot of choir
• Instrumentalist, finishing opening bars of the song
• Singer, as begins singing
• Second, different shot of singer, a bit tighter
• Instrumentalist (brief)
• Singer again
• Choir, as begins singing
• Singer, tight

In such a scenario, shots of the singer last longer, and cutaways of the band are shorter. If the choir begins a solo section or an instrumentalist begins a solo, then the focus of the song shifts from the singer. Always return to the action after one or two brief cutaways. Like any effective storytelling, the object is to build to a climax over the course of the story.

Be aware that there is meaning in various shots. Alfred Hitchcock was a master at creating meaning in shot structure. In the classic film *North by Northwest*, there is a single shot that captures the essence of the film's story. As Cary Grant's character leaves the United Nations building upon realizing that he is being pursued for reasons he does not understand, his feeling of utter helplessness is perfectly captured by the extreme bird's-eye shot from atop the building. He looks like a little ant, and he feels like one, too.

Conversely, shots from underneath create a sense of power in the subject. Clint Eastwood's *The Man with No Name*, in Sergio Leone's spaghetti westerns, is often captured from underneath, with plenty of backlight. The large, silhouetted figure looks quite menacing.

Watch late-night television. At the end of most shows is a featured musical selection by a contemporary artist. Notice both the types and lengths of shots, the shot selection by the director, and how shots are ordered to communicate the feel of the action to the viewer.

## Language

Like any new form of communication, digital media has its own particular language, and this time I mean it literally. There are very specific buzzwords and jargon that media people need to know to communicate effectively, and it is important to teach these words throughout the ministry. (See the bonus materials at www.thewiredchurch2.com for a "command list.") In the heat of the moment, if a director has to call for an unplanned shot, it is a lot easier to say, "Take four" than it is to say, "Put the, you know, the-thing-up!" In addition, although it is best to work with static teams, for whatever reason there are times in which directors or team members must switch weekends. Universal jargon ensures proper communication, regardless of the team composition.

## Timing

Timing separates a person who can hit the right button or call the right shot from the one who communicates a story through images. Pay close attention to subtle aspects of the service. When are short dissolves better, and when are long dissolves more appropriate? If your projector displays its input mode on the screen before the congregation, be wary of how switching the projector mode from "Video 1" to "RGB 1" will flash those words on the screen, erasing the work of the Holy Spirit in midair. Be aware of these little details, and strive to match the atmosphere being created by music, lighting, and the spoken word.

Anticipate cues before they come, so that graphics occur just prior to the cue, not with it or after. Always err on the front end of the cue. The same applies for videos. Always roll tape or cue the computer in such a way that the clip begins as the speaker is finishing a sentence. Remember TV culture: how long is the black space between commercials and programming in broadcast television? The space between media elements should be short, as well.

It is also more pleasing to time dissolves so that they occur in tandem with live elements. For example, in a sermon, make camera transitions and graphic incues and outcues during breath pauses, rather than in the middle of a sentence, for smoothness, or less distraction.

## Video Clips

Depending on your technical configuration, video clips may be played off DVD or videotape, through a computer, or directly from your computer's hard drive.

If the clip is on physical media such as DVD, make sure you cue all tapes before worship! Or, at least, cue all clips at least two minutes before its scheduled airing in the sermon.

As learned in the school of hard knocks, when using a remote at any time during a live production, after use, set down the remote to avoid any inadvertent finger-twitching that may cause the clip to stop.

# CHAPTER 14
# SPIRITUAL COACHING AND LEADERSHIP

On equal footing with technical proficiency is the spiritual leadership that a director can provide. The media minister, paid or unpaid, is a pastor responsible for nurturing the presence of the Holy Spirit in the lives of the team members.

Outside of worship, this nurturing involves many actions.

Make regular contact with all your team members, regardless of the degree of involvement or commitment. Ask accountability questions, such as, are you reading for Bible study? Are you praying? How is your personal life? Are your relationships healthy? Do you tithe? Give them specific books that they can read and study. Answer spiritual questions if the need is present, and be available to recognize that need.

Find out if this is your team member's primary ministry. Are they serving regularly? If not, where else do they serve? And how often or how much? Help regulate that kind of activity, depending on the individual, to keep your team members from overextending themselves and burning out. For some, balance can be an issue, while others could be exhorted to greater amounts of giving. Hold them accountable to service, not merely to technology.

Organize occasional events as suited to your team. Make some gatherings social and others based in spiritual growth. The emphasis on spiritual nurture in the media ministry team depends on church size (how many other types of small groups are providing this nurture?) and on the personal chemistry of the small group that is devoted to media ministry.

In team gatherings, interject often the spiritual impact of what a media team does: cast vision. For example, point out persons in the congregation who are affected by what media ministry is doing. Talk about the importance of the ministry. Pray as a group prior to the event, for the specific purpose of the task at hand and also to encourage or develop awareness of the ministry as a place for transforming others' lives, and for personal transformation.

Do fun things with the team. Take care of them while they are working by making sure food and water are available. Encourage them often while serving. Compliment their victories, and coach their defeats. When appropriate, take breaks from tasks at hand for fellowship.

For many in media ministry, this small group is their only means of accountability and transformation. Build for the future on this, their only training in the life of the body of Christ.

# EXERTING SPIRITUAL LEADERSHIP DURING PRODUCTIONS

When team members do not execute their task properly, which is an inevitable part of any live production, the director must be able to correct the team member in a Christlike way while ensuring that the task is completed well. This leader walks a tightrope between the poles of excellence and edification. Remember that each illustration or media piece may be critical to an unchurched person's understanding of the gospel. To be excellent is to not keep media elements that are only "good enough," dropping them from the production if necessary.

A tightly woven community of volunteers is one in which every team member realizes his or her contribution to the whole. This creates a sense of purpose that leads to finer production and fulfilled servants.

Furthermore, the director must be able to take charge of every situation over the headsets. Sometimes it is the tendency of team members to lose focus and begin chatting about irrelevant things. While occasional chatter may be good for building community, it should never interfere with the task at hand. It is the director's job to monitor its status, and to maintain the group's focus. When deciding what is an appropriate level of chatter, it is better to err on the side of silence.

# CHOOSING A DIRECTOR AND MEDIA MINISTRY LEADERS

The proper understanding of the live production as part of the ministry is what separates the director from other ministry positions and from the secular media industries. The director is the hardest role to fill because the individual must have the technical expertise to execute the production and the compassion to do it with grace and encouragement. Either ability alone is dangerous; the former because the ministry will see a body count, the latter because the ministry will never achieve the level of excellence required to communicate the message effectively.

In mature media ministries, directors should be individually selected for apprenticeship. An apprentice will work one-on-one with a current director or media ministry leader for several live runs (months), learning every aspect of the position. Apprentices are evaluated by the current director, other directors on the team, and by the coordinating pastor during the training phase to determine if and when the apprentice is ready to assume the leadership role.

If you are the first pastor or volunteer media minister at your church to attempt multisensory worship, it will be several months before it is possible to train an apprentice. Your training can come from the following sources:

- Find another congregation in your region, where you can occasionally seek the help or advice of a willing mentor who is pursuing media ministry.
- Attend a media ministry conference (such as Creative Worship and Design Matters, two one-day seminars presented by Midnight Oil Productions).
- Take a course in videography at the local community college or technical institute.
- Pursue long-distance learning over the Internet; for example, through trade magazine sites, which often have feature articles that cover use and application of technology.

# THE POWER OF THE MEDIA TEAM

Louis is a team member on the media ministry team in his church. He grew up in church and had a number of negative experiences with church during his teenage years. While aware of Christ, his faith remained mostly intellectual and was perhaps wounded by the actions of others.

While in his twenties, Louis did not attend church often. Eventually, he returned and began to operate a camera once a month. Through the encouragement of directors in the media ministry, he gradually began to take on more of a committed role in the ministry, serving not just once but entire weekends, often two times per month.

One summer the team invited him to become a director. Louis was hesitant out of caution about the responsibilities, both in production and in spiritual leadership, but he accepted. Over the course of the summer he directed a number of weekends. The transition was not always smooth; one weekend the first service went so poorly that he wanted to quit out of frustration and feelings of inadequacy. But the media minister would not let him, and he improved in skill and leadership as the months went by.

Beyond the technical requirements of the position, however, through the position Louis had begun to accept God's calling to spiritual leadership. He began a Bible study group in response to a need within the media ministry.

Louis is like the rest of us, a work in progress, growing into Christ's likeness. And it has been through involvement and, eventually, leadership in media ministry that he is being transformed from a disillusioned teenager into a leader for Christ's church.

Media ministry changes lives, and that is our objective.

# CHAPTER 15
# PREPARATION FOR THE BIG EVENT

An understanding of the design and production process as well as development of the volunteer teams has given you the means to create a Wired Church. Review the process using this guideline below, which offers a sample outline for one week in the life of a media ministry.

These steps show what might happen in a mature environment as you gain experience. If you are just starting, the basic steps remain but with fewer complex activities.

## STEP 1: BRAINSTORMING PROCESS

- Identify the one great idea or theme for the weekend and the metaphor to illustrate it. For more insight into thematic worship development and the use of metaphor, see *Digital Storytellers: The Art of Communicating the Gospel in Worship* (Abingdon Press, 2002).
- Begin thinking about how to visually represent the chosen theme and metaphor for the weekend. For more insight into creating images that convey meaning, see chapter 7, Visual Preaching and Worship Planning, and also read *Design Matters: Creating Powerful Imagery for Worship* (Abingdon Press, 2006).

- Identify possible preproduced video clips, either produced by a film studio or one of the online marketplaces for worship media. See Bonus Materials section at www.thewiredchurch2.com for a list of production companies and retailers that offer preproduced worship media.
- Explore possibilities for original media, including still images and video. See pages 58–67 for a list of ways to use media in worship.
- For an original video, make a script or storyboard for specific shots that will be needed for the video. Coordinate talent and any production personnel, a location (if necessary), and all necessary equipment.
- For original graphic images, research and sketch rough drawings for primary and supporting worship images. (Note: If producing both still images and video, match them if possible.)

## STEP 2: ACQUIRE ELEMENTS

- Rent and view films for any movie clips, as needed.
- Purchase and download preproduced videos from the Internet as needed.
- Shoot videos on location as needed.
- Finalize first draft of primary worship graphic.
- Log or digitize video clips from a shoot.
- Choose a music bed for the video.
- Shoot, scan, digitize, or create graphic elements.

## STEP 3: EDITING AND PREPARATION

- Edit video.
- With at least a rough draft of the sermon complete, meet with the preacher to review image possibilities.
- Identify a few (interpretive) illustrations for the sermon and coordinate the collection of any additional needed graphic elements.
- Create a technical script based on the sermon notes, outlining all media cues in their respective locations.
- Key in song lyrics and scripture text and import and compose all media elements into presentation software. For more information on available software for presenting media in worship, see the Presentation Software review in the Bonus Materials section at www.thewiredchurch2.com.
- Confirm with the volunteer crew the schedule for their service time. Be ready in case of emergency to help schedule someone else. Consider using a service such as Yahoo's Calendar to contact people automatically and receive RSVPs of their planned presence.

- Review the order of worship scripts. Send scripts for worship ahead of time to directors by e-mail. Consider organizing the service with two distinct scripts:
  1. Order of worship, which is the same script handed to everyone involved with the worship celebration, from band members to dramatists, and sometimes to the congregation. It contains all the elements of worship, as well as dialogue for any prewritten elements, such as calls to worship, sacramental rituals, dramas, and so forth. This dialogue is an important cueing tool for the director.
  2. Technical script, which is a structured interpretation of all media cues, such as "video here" or "lights down on prayer," and the preacher's message, with cues and descriptions of media elements. The sermon script is created during the same weekday meeting that determines which graphics are made.

# STEP 4: FINAL PRESENTATION AND REHEARSAL

- Meet with the preacher prior to the first worship service to finalize the graphic images and their cues. Often, incues and outcues change or graphics are moved or dropped depending on further sermon development. Have the preacher conduct a mock run-through of the sermon, hitting on every graphic or video illustration. During the run-through the director should listen along for unique ways that the preacher might indicate or cue a media piece. Additionally, specific incues or outcues may not be listed on the sermon script. In this event, ask the speaker and make notes accordingly. As with all extemporaneous speaking, sometimes the preacher may adjust his or her sermon from what is written. In that event, the director must rely on knowledge of the sermon and key points the speaker might mention, as indicated in the script. Every speaker is different. Learn each person's unique way of presenting and interacting with media elements. Stay on your toes at all times; as with all live production, there is no telling what might happen!
- Use the checklist (located in the website Bonus Materials), to ensure that all media is properly prepared for worship. Sometimes equipment gets used for other purposes during the week, particularly in smaller and less-established environments. Check to ensure that all equipment is configured properly and that switches are set to their proper positions.
- Make any necessary eleventh-hour changes.

- Conduct the technical rehearsal. The technical rehearsal is a mock run of the entire service with all entities participating, and prevents your first worship event from being a run-through. (As we like to say at seminars, don't make the first service the tech rehearsal!) A separate technical coordinator, who must integrate media with the other elements of the event, might run the meeting. This allows the media director to focus entirely on the details of the big picture. Make sure you project all graphics—including videos, text, and announcements—during this time for confirmation or adjustment. It is common to encounter typographical errors or poor image quality during technical rehearsal. Run through key points and transitions at least twice, with all relevant parties present.
- Ask questions. The director is responsible for all content and transitions on the screen during worship. Again, pay particular note to transitions. During the production, verbally state what events are ahead. Keep the entire crew aware of where the service is going. This keeps everyone in the loop and not merely a robot at your mercy. Function as a liaison with other team members, including the stage director and other media areas, to ensure that good communication is recurring. Feelings can be easily hurt during an intense production; most of the time this is through lack of communication. For unpaid team members, don't verbally disagree with a paid staff decision if there are other unpaid members present who could interpret this as dissension.

Worship begins!

PART FOUR

# MASTERING THE
# TECHNOLOGY

# CHAPTER 16

# A STORY ON GETTING STARTED

## ONE PASTOR'S STORY, TWO DIFFERENT CHURCHES

I don't come to church to watch TV!" snapped a board member the night Bill Myers made a short presentation on the use of digital media in worship to his church leadership.

In every story of introducing Change in worship—"change" usually seems to come with a capital C—there are going to be some challenges. For some local churches, change is more difficult than for others. For Pastor Myers, the challenge was in developing like-minded lay leadership. He knew it was vital to having any success with implementing digital media in worship. To achieve this goal, he also knew that the perceptions of choice and ownership were crucial.

His strategy that night was to sidestep the issue of change by avoiding the word altogether. In a presentation, he told his neighborhood congregation that if they "wanted to maintain their visibility in a changing culture, they would need to add video projection capabilities to the sanctuary." While many tend to resist change, he says, most are open to adding something.

After his initial presentation, Myers didn't bring up the matter again. Four months went by. Then, one night in a board meeting, someone said, "Bill, we think we need to start talking about adding video projection to worship." Again, he responded with choice and ownership, quickly outlining a proposal with three elements, at a total cost of $18,000, then leaving the decision to them.

The church accepted all three.

Bill Myers, a United Methodist pastor in Michigan, knew a little about introducing change. Bill took two churches outside the usual contemporary model and brought them into the digital age through a deft combination of political, technical, and creative skill. Some people experience difficulty getting one "contemporary" church to use digital media effectively. Bill did it at two "traditional" churches, both of which would be considered a challenge to most. In the process, he is destroying the old perception that it takes a large, wealthy, suburban church to "do media."

The three-part system Bill proposed (from 2004):

- A single 1500 ANSI lumen projector, which accepts an XGA signal from a Macintosh G4 computer. The projection screen is motorized and is always retracted when not in use. The Macintosh uses Grass Roots Software's SundayPlus in the dual-monitor mode with two 17" CRT monitors in the booth.
- For production concerns, Formac Studio's $300 TVR converts analog video to DV streams, which are then captured using either iMovie or Final Cut Pro, for use in SundayPlus.
- A Sony pan-tilt-zoom remotely controlled camera, placed on a beam about 10 feet in front of the chancel, projects events within the service that are difficult for some members of the congregation to see, such as the children's message, baptisms, solos, and so forth.
- The video and audio are run through an RF modulator ($20) so a TV signal can be sent to the nursery.
- A small mixer sends audio from the computer/DVD/VCR setup to the sanctuary's main audio mixer board.

The total cost of this system, at $15,000, came in well under Bill's proposal.

Even though Bill described himself as a "techie masquerading as a pastor" (he has since passed away), he didn't lead his churches into digital media out of his own passions and hobbies. He did it out of a passion to proclaim the gospel. He stated, "Gone are the days when people received their information, or participated in worship, primarily through the written word. Not only is the visual medium becoming primary for many people, it also allows for more versatility and creativity. The concept Midnight Oil teaches about 'redeeming the culture' is key to this point."[1]

Shortly after the system was installed, Bill accepted a new local church appointment. The night he was introduced to his new congregation, a trustee whispered in his ear, "We figured out where the screen can go!" After accepting a new charge, Bill was relieved to find his new lay leadership to be more like-minded. However, he soon discovered that the second church had its own set of challenges. The problems now weren't with vision but with money.

The congregation, which was founded in 1833, worships in a 1907 structure in downtown Battle Creek, Michigan. The roof needed repairs, the telephone lines were decrepit, the sprinkler system wasn't functioning, the fire marshal had just informed the church that they had to add more emergency lighting, and the congregation wanted air-conditioning in the sanctuary. Not to mention his parsonage needed work.

Into this environment Bill wanted to spend money on digital media in worship. To make matters more difficult, because of the sanctuary's oval shape and recent restoration, care was needed to create not one but two screens, and to integrate the technology so that it was not obtrusive to the classic architecture.

His solution: to kick off a $100,000 capital finds campaign six weeks into his tenure, with $25,000 earmarked for video projection. The media proposal (from 2005):

- Two 3000 ANSI lumen projectors hide behind pre-existing PA speakers and project onto retractable screens. One 2000 ANSI lumen projector shoots directly onto the back wall and functions as a stage monitor.
- An added video booth at the balcony level houses a Macintosh G4 with dual 17" CRT monitors and SundayPlus presentation software. An Extron scan converter converts the Macintosh's RGB signal to S-Video, which is mixed along with the VCR/DVD player into a Panasonic video switcher ($1,200).
- Two Canon GL2 cameras on basic tripods project live worship activity to the screens.

- As with the first proposal, the video and audio are run through an RF modulator ($20) so a TV signal can be sent to the nursery and throughout the building. Formac Studio's $300 TVR converts analog video to DV streams for editing, and a small mixer sends audio from the computer/DVD/VCR setup to the sanctuary's main audio mixer board.

Bill used S-Video in the second installation because it is cheaper on long signal paths than a computer signal. He explained, "The four-input switcher allows us to have immediate access to computer video, video cameras, DVD, and VCR, and to send these signals to the projectors without any synchronization problems." The output of the switcher runs into two special S-Video distribution amplifiers, which were custom built by the contractor. This amplified signal runs to the two main (front) projectors and the rear-facing projector. Bill explained,

> This system was designed so that the rear-facing projector can be "split off" from the main signal. We use it in this mode when we are doing a musical or drama so that it can be used as a teleprompter. Of course, using it this way means that a second computer needs to be added to the system to drive the rear projector. This feature has allowed us to improve the quality of our productions while at the same time reducing the number of rehearsals.

The total cost of this system was $34,000, with under $1,000 spent on the control booth.

Bill's background was what you might expect for a "techie pastor." He got a ham radio license before he got a driver's license. In seminary, he used his radio to communicate with missionaries in jungle outposts. As he began to minister in a local church, he found himself helping other churches with their PA system problems, recycling old parts with the help of church volunteers to prevent clueless pastors from getting taken by A/V dealers.

Somewhere along his ministry path, someone suggested to Bill that he had a nice voice for narration. He wasn't your typical talent, though. Instead of reading the script and leaving the studio, he would hang around and observe. This led him into the world of image and video editing.

Bill acknowledged that it's unusual to be gifted in technical stuff while at the same time grasping the necessary elements of pastoral care. None of that in his view, though, made his story special. He questioned the difference between the challenges he faced in pastoring century-old, mainline churches and what churches of any style face today. He said, "I believe the challenges that churches experience today have little to do with geography or denomination. What touches each church is the changing American culture. Most specifically, I believe that the way people assimilate information is a key." The most urban, innovative church faces the same challenges as the most rural and traditional.

Bill Myers believed that anyone, given the proper advice and guidance, can install a system on their own. All of us are in "challenging" situations. Such is the nature of ministry in our digital age. The two most commonly used rationales for avoiding this challenge are lack of church vision and lack of money. Bill demonstrated in two successive pastoral appointments that neither are truly obstacles for those who have the passion and desire to communicate the gospel.

# CHAPTER 17

# LESSONS ON THE USE
# OF TECHNOLOGY

Shortly after my third child, Joslyn, arrived my wife and I decided to research the specifics of acquiring a backyard playground set. Unlike the rickety, "V"-shaped contraptions of my own childhood, playgrounds now offer the luxury of elaborate redwood and cedar forts and commercial-grade equipment in kids' own backyards. If you are unfamiliar with the world of "play systems" but have seen large, wooden background structures with colorful roofs peeking over privacy fences in local neighborhoods, then you know what we discovered. While we appreciated the increased attention to safety, we were a little less enthusiastic about the price tag. A modest system with installation costs upward of $4,000, and top of the line units cost over $30,000!

One day I discovered a local discount center offering a generic brand, redwood, prefabricated playground, made at the same factory as the high-dollar ones, for only $1,300. It said "Assembly Required," but I thought, how hard can it be?

I started work on it the Thursday before Easter. Let's just say that Christ died, was buried, and rose again while I was outside matching slot A to tab B. It was like putting together discount furniture, but ten times worse. My power tools ran out of juice; my toddlers confiscated various bolts; I got sunburned; it rained.

Through it all I kept at it, because for all of the trouble, good tools and good instructions allowed me to keep my eye on the bigger idea of creating a fun outdoor place for my kids to play on at home. Now, having finished the project, I can stand out back and swing the kids as a proud daddy while the kids jump and play.

Over the course of the project I used a number of tools of varying quality to accomplish the task at hand. Occasionally, I even used things not intended to be playground-building tools: a butter knife, a pair of scissors, a pocketknife. Except for the first time I squeezed the trigger of the power drill, I don't think I once stopped to marvel at the tools I was using. The focus wasn't the tools. It was the project. Similarly, technology is neither the purpose nor the reason for media ministry, nor is it the most important aspect of the ministry.

Ideas drive technology—not the other way around. Don't confuse the means with the end.

# 1. FOCUS ON CREATIVITY AND DON'T WORRY ABOUT TECHNOLOGY

Since the beginning of radio, TV, and film, inventive storytellers have used makeshift means to create other times and places. In the early 1960s, a teenage Steven Spielberg created a feature-length war film using amazing special effects tools such as two-by-fours and mounds of dirt. His peer George Lucas later made *Star Wars* on a B-movie budget. Even as studios now spend incredible amounts of money on computerized special effects, and superhero blockbusters encourage behemoth production budgets, digital media is becoming democratized. Network television and national ad firms are using fan-generated videos. The makers of YouTube went from working in a garage to selling their company for over a billion dollars in two years because they captured the lightning in the bottle that has been democratized media. At local churches, I have seen incredible storytelling from youth groups who were using nothing more than a cheap digital video camera and free editing software.

So jump in. Don't wait for the prices to come down or the technology to get easier. These are excuses that short-circuit the world from hearing the gospel in indigenous language. The time and resources required to make that happen are a part of doing ministry in the digital age.

## 2. DON'T LET THE TAIL WAG THE DOG

I almost gave up on the playground when my power drill's battery expired. It is at first devastating to lose your only good tool in the heat of the project. That was, until I began poking around and discovered a few old, beat-up tools that served the same purpose. If one tool causes the shutdown of the entire project, the tail is wagging.

I sometimes read media trade magazines and surf technical forums online to keep up with the latest trends and developments. Trade journals are good sources for product reviews, technology updates, and creative applications. Generally, they are required reading for anyone wishing to work in media, particularly in the professional vacuum that occurs while working in media in a local congregation. In one issue, the feature article proclaimed with huge, edgy type: "Content Is King!" That writer's epiphany may seem obvious, but he had simply fallen into the trap so common to technology users, the trap of putting media technology before the messages that it is designed to send. Often, new technology is a solution without a problem. Make sure your purchases are driven by your vision, not the other way around.

Technology doesn't drive ideas, or at least it shouldn't. Ideas drive technology.[1]

Don't be like the fellow who likes to collect tools, who would show off his latest closet-sized red toolbox of shiny wrenches and sockets, but oddly never seems to build anything with those tools. Tools for him are about status: a real man possesses a loaded red toolbox, ready for any project, no matter how large. There is no point in having highly specialized computers, plus video hardware and software, unless you have a clear idea of its intended use. Just like you never know what tools you'll need until you begin the project and read the manual, the types of equipment needed to begin a media ministry depend thoroughly on what it is that you want to accomplish.

So if you've skipped straight to the technical section of this book, go back to the beginning and read the chapter on mission!

## 3. TECHNOLOGY IS NEVER STATE-OF-THE-ART BUT IT'S NEVER OBSOLETE, EITHER

The playground utilized a neat synthesis of old and new technology to fuse together its parts. Standard screws were housed in plastic casings, which could then be inserted into preset indentions in the wood. This enabled us to access the screws while the unit was partially assembled; yet it concealed them from view when it was done.

As with these inventive casings, digital media is always a synthesis of old and new forms, both conceptually and pragmatically. Like other industries in North American culture, advancement in media is driven by technology, which is mandated by commerce. If we can now make something so good it will never break down, the best way to turn the crank of commerce is to create a new and better version of the same thing. This is why we continually see the latest and greatest quickly become the oldest and moldiest. (Of course, any experienced computer user can refute the idea that newer is always better. When Microsoft upgraded its word processing application, Word, from version 5.1 to 6.0 in the 1990s, it alienated many users by replacing a sleek, usable interface with a cumbersome, clunky one that was so busy it left little room for composition and took up to three times as much space on their hard drives. Internet chat groups sprang up denouncing the software and offering hints on how to keep the old version viable. Strangely, some would say they did the same thing again with Vista.)

Old does not necessarily mean obsolete. There are many ways in which older tools can retain their effectiveness. While I was an intern at CBS Television City Hollywood in 1995, I was amazed to see the original videotape technology still in use. The first videotape machines, wall-sized units from the early 1950s that used videotape reels two inches thick and as large as a small automobile wheel, required extensive manual threading to operate. These ancient video machines were being used for a special archiving project in the basement of the facility! There are always uses for available technology. As the first wave of equipment purchases slowly get replaced with newer technologies, reassign the old to new uses: use it as a training device for youth, or as a mission project to enable work-program recipients to become literate in digital media. Technology becomes synthesized with itself as it takes on new forms.

On the other hand, the fact that old stuff usually continues to work doesn't mean one should neglect to budget for new technologies. Although there are times in which technology is a solution without a problem, there are times in which the problems exist for a long time without a specific solution. Many congregations will allocate special dollars, such as a grant, for equipment purchases, but fail to include media as a viable ministry item for budgeting. To put it frankly, the expense of digital media is just the cost of "doing business" in this culture.

Thus, the media minister must constantly maintain the delicate balance of utilizing existing equipment while projecting future needs (and costs) against emerging technology. How difficult is that? New technology may be the media person's siren song. Extreme caution is urged, as there are many distracting toys.

# 4. COST IS RELATIVE

One of the first, and never-ending, things you may hear from a congregation that is contemplating digital media is its insane cost. Professional video users tend to compound this perception by referring to the sort of equipment video production studios are purchasing, which tend to cost upward of six figures annually. Further, this perception is compounded by early efforts of local churches in media ministry, which were invariably about broadcast and not in-house production. Broadcast is a terribly expensive venture.

Two principles apply: advancements in technology are always initially expensive, and as more users purchase the technology and it mutates through various revisions, the cost of production drops dramatically. This is the law of supply and demand.

This is one of the greatest benefits of pursuing ministry in the language of the culture. Since most of the culture speaks the same language, cost per unit becomes inexpensive. At one time, viewing a motion picture outside of a movie theater, which is the industry's established distribution system, meant contacting a nontheatrical distribution center, paying a licensing fee, waiting for the film in the mail, setting up a projectionist's booth at your facility, and so on. It was so difficult that it was rarely done. Now a feature film is viewable on our home theater systems, on our computer screens, in our mobile media players, and even in our phones. The cost and hassle is restricted to a rental or a download and a couple of bucks.

Furthermore, a computer with a tenth of the current processing power was at one time ten times as expensive as it is now. Moore's Law (named after Gordon Moore, cofounder of Intel) has basically held true for forty years: computer processing power doubles in size and speed every two years. This pace has been good to consumers in the form of falling prices.

On the other hand, it is becoming increasingly expensive to speak a language that is no longer spoken by the majority of the culture. The cost of working in 8mm film has become very expensive in relation to DVD or digital files because it is so hard to find a processing facility and maintain adequate projection equipment.

The lifetime cost of media hardware is becoming increasingly negligible. A home stereo system is analogous: phonographs needed replacement needles and cleaner for vinyl LPs, and cassette tape decks need their paths cleaned (often by a professional), but CD players require none of the above, as their primary operating device is a laser, and even better, digital files don't even have to fool with physical media that may get scratched or damaged.

All this is to say, it does not take rocket scientists to produce media, and they don't need NASA's budget, either. Democratization of knowledge and technique is good. The B-side to this, however, is that certain technological basics must be met in both the production and presentation of electronic media. These basics are outlined in the following chapters in a series of steps, or phases. First, however, you may benefit from a short lesson on the tools of media.

CHAPTER 18

# TECHNICAL BASICS

On the road, on the phone, and across the Internet I have heard the same cry from churches of all sizes and persuasions: "Help! Only a professional can understand all of this technology!"

Fear not. There has always been a symbiotic relationship between art and technology. For example, Renaissance artists were expert technicians at emerging technologies in paints, and at creating new paints to accomplish their creative visions. A few basic descriptions will enable you to make your way through trade magazines, which is the best way to increase your fluency and confidence.

So, here are a few snappy answers to some good questions.

## VIDEO

### What Exactly Is Video?

Video, like film, is actually a series of still images that run past the eyes at the quick rate of thirty frames per second. Each still frame of video is composed of a number of horizontal lines. In standard-definition video, the number of these lines is not to exceed 525, per national standards.

Each of these thirty stills per image is actually composed of two **fields**, or half images that occur sixty times per second, and are **interlaced**, like two hands doing the childhood game of "here's the church, here's the steeple." High-definition video, on the other hand, occurs within one of three standards: 1080i (or 1080 interlaced lines of data), 720p (or **720 progressively** drawn lines of data, like on a computer monitor), or 1080p—the highest quality and most expensive option being the last.

| Lines of Resolution | |
| --- | --- |
| The number of lines that compose an NTSC signal. A rating unit for determining the quality of a signal. | |
| Maximum number of lines in standard-definition (NTSC) video, established 50 years ago | 525, or 480 plus 45 lines for black and data |
| Actual number of lines in a typical standard definition NTSC broadcast | 330 |
| Number of lines in full HD monitors | 720 progressive or 1080 interlaced or progressive |
| Number of lines a typical standard-definition industrial camera can capture | 740 |
| Approximate number of lines in VHS videotape | 240 |
| Approximate number of lines in standard DVD discs | 500-540 |
| Approximate number of lines in Blu-ray high definition DVD discs | 1080 |

## How Do I Acquire Images?

In the early days, a complex system of tubes was used, but today the acquisition of images is a data transmission process in which images are converted from the lens of a camera to recordable information through a **computer chip**. Consumer-level cameras do this through a single composite chip (a one-chip camera). Industrial and broadcast cameras use three computer chips, one for each primary video color: red, green, and blue. The better video comes from three-chip cameras.

## So, the Number of Chips Determines the Quality of Video?

If it were merely up to the chips, all three-chip video would look as good as it does in the basement of CBS. But other technical variables have an impact. One variable is the aforementioned lines of resolution. Although 720 progressive is the high-definition broadcast standard, the amount of actual lines of resolution in an image actually depends on the quality of the equipment. Though it is not the only barometer of a signal's quality, it is a good one. A typical standard-definition industrial camera is capable of up to 740 lines of resolution; a typical industrial HD camera captures 720 lines (progressive) or 1080 lines (interlaced). But, the quality of a video image shrinks when digitally compressed. It's almost like squeezing everyone in the Bronx through the George Washington Bridge on the way to New Jersey. The best digital compression schemes (or **codecs**) are when all the lanes are working, even though it is still a tight fit; the worst codecs are when they're doing construction on half the lanes during rush hour.

## The Wide World of Cameras

Cameras range in quality from the little handheld camcorders found in consumer electronics stores to $250,000 broadcast studio cameras that never leave the cool confines of a basement studio. Basically, cameras fall into three categories: consumer, industrial (or corporate), and broadcast. In addition, there is a gray area between the first two, commonly called "prosumer." Although there are many technical differences among the categories, the obvious dividing line is price.

Comparable technical specifications in cameras include: the number of processing chips; the number of pixels that the computer chip(s) can process; the rating for low light conditions; and the **signal-to-noise** ratio, which is measured in decibels (dBs). Signal to noise is the amount of pure video the camera captures in each frame versus the amount of spurious information, or noise, it captures.

## Explain the Different Types of Video Capture to Me

In the days of videotape, a videographer had to worry about which **format** among many on which to shoot. **Mini-DV**, a standard-definition format that became popular in the late 1990s, is proving to be the final tape format. It has been a transition format, where although the media is still a cassette tape, the recording on the tape is digital and not analog like with former formats including Betacam, SVHS, and Hi8.

Newer cameras are equipped with both hard drives and mini-DV cassette drives. This transitory phase is analogous to buying a car with a CD and a tape player stereo. The cassette drive is handy to have, but gets used little. The trend is toward recording directly to hard drives. With the hard drive, the issue then becomes ensuring that the codec used to capture the raw footage is compatible with the right editing software.

Hard drives are resolution independent; that is, for HD-equipped cameras, it is simply a setting in the menu to switch for the videographer to record standard-definition or high-definition video footage. New shooters don't know how easy they've got it!

## What Is the Difference between All the Various Cables?

Analog video cables still have a use, especially in a church environment, where there may be need to run signals to monitors or mixers.

There are really only three basic types of analog video cables. The most common is the **Composite** cable, which contains the entire video signal and has either an **RCA** (like the traditional home stereo or DVD player) or **BNC** (round, metal, and latching) connector. Composite is the least-expensive, lowest-quality type of cable.

The second type, **S-Video** cable, separates the video signal into luminance and chrominance, or brightness/contrast and color saturation/hue. The most common S-Video connector is a weak four-pin plastic casing. The casing doesn't do a very good job of protecting the pins, which get damaged often. Another type of S-Video connector is the YC, which is actually two BNC connectors split from a single cable, one for luminance (Y) and one for chrominance (C). S-Video cable carries a better signal than composite because of its ability to separate luminance and chrominance.

The best-quality analog video signal is called **Component**, which is a single signal that has been broken into a number of individual wires, each with its own BNC-style connector on the end. The parts are red, green, blue, vertical sync, and horizontal sync, with "sync" for synchronization, keeping the parts of the signal locked together. Component is the best-quality cable, as it separates each color into its individual spectrum and is able to maintain complete chromatic integrity.

A third type of cable connection is **RF**, which is a composite video and audio signal connector. It is the same as the basic wire that most people receive from their local cable service, and is handy for wiring together multiple TVs/VCRs and monitoring workstations around a facility or campus.

## Lighting Is Way Over My Head

The number-one rule about lighting: make sure you have some.

The number-two rule: make sure there is more light in front of the subject than behind the subject. This is called the **key** light. A basic attention to detail on light surroundings goes a long way toward professional-quality video.

Inexpensive camera-mounted lights are available at many consumer video outlets. These suffice for grittier productions such as an "On-the-Street" video. Professional field-production lighting kits can be purchased for about $1,000 and do a wonderful job of spreading even light across a subject. In the absence of a budget, however, it is possible to get away with such handy tools as shop worklights and incandescent lamps. Regardless of the type of light used, follow the basic three-part procedure below:

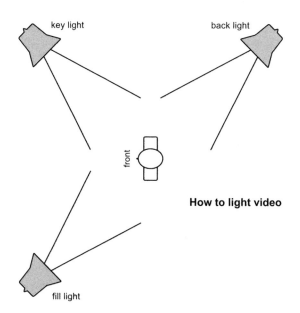

**How to light video**

# COMPUTERS

Computers are a whole world in and of themselves, and the basics for getting around in a PC or Macintosh have become prerequisite for not just media ministry but just about any kind of program ministry. Due to its complicated nature, the best method for learning about computers is through a separate publication, of which there are many on the market. Here I can answer a few questions regarding the graphics production aspect of computer technology.

## The Difference between a Computer and a TV Is . . . ?

The images generated from computers and in video are inherently different. A computer signal is called an **RGB** signal, a technical anagram for the highly esoteric industry terms Red, Green, and Blue. RGB signals are noninterlaced, or progressive, which as discussed means that the computer writes the screen line-by-line from top to bottom and then starts over again, many times per second. (In fact, the monitor rating, Hz, indicates how many times per second the computer writes the noninterlaced display. So a 75Hz monitor draws a full screen of lines seventy-five times every second.) **Video**, on the other hand, has in its final form traditionally been an analog signal, and must conform to the guidelines set by the NTSC, or North American Television Standards Committee. (There are actually different standards for France and the rest of the world, called SECAM and PAL, respectively. As usual, we North Americans do things our own way!) Video is interlaced, as indicated above, so it draws its lines alternatively. Newer digital television signals, either in standard- or high-definition, can be interlaced or progressive.

## How Do I Get from One to the Other?

Since the two signals are different, to be displayed together or in each other's realm, the computer signal must be converted to video, or vice versa. To convert from a computer signal to a video signal, it must be changed from noninterlaced to interlaced, by a process called **scan conversion**. "Scan converters" (little boxes with computer and video ins and outs), or video cards that accomplish the same function, are an indispensable part of any technical configuration involving both computers and video. The opposite conversion, from video to computer, is done in a live setting through the use of a **scalar**. Newer mixers can handle these conversions all within a single box, so a user can plug anything from a computer to an old VCR to a new HD camera all into the same box for live mixing.

High-definition, as mentioned, is changing this neat dichotomy, but for the foreseeable future all but the most expensive sanctuary media systems will still have to decide if they want to base the system on the RGB signal or the video signal, as they are different and must be converted one to another to work together.

## What about Getting Images into a Computer for Editing?

There are three primary ways to place an image or series of images inside a computer, a process commonly known as "digitizing."

Flatbed **scanners** take a snapshot of a two-dimensional image, often a photograph, and reproduce the image within the computer. Scanning is the best means of digitizing flat materials such as slides and 35mm photographs.

**Digital still cameras**, which have become fairly ubiquitous, serve the same function as a traditional 35mm camera, without the need for film. Images are stored onto a small disc that can then be transferred into a computer system. Digital cameras are ideal for photographing three-dimensional objects for image manipulating and compositing.

Videotape from a video camera can be digitized into a computer through special video capture cards or through data transfer from digital videotape. As mentioned, videotape is fading, and soon all acquisition will be done through hard drives.

## What Is Dpi, and Why Should I Care?

"Dpi" is dots per inch, a term coined during print days to refer to the number of **pixels**, or little dots on a display, that comprise an inch of ink on paper. Although dpi in the print world may be 150, or 300, or much higher for color reproduction, the highest dpi necessary for electronic images is 72. Anything more is wasted space.

The standard size for a digital image is dependent on the projector being used. For example, an **XGA** projector, like its monitor counterpart, handles 1024x768 images. So any graphics built for this specific projector should be made according to these specifications. Unlike print, there are a maximum number of pixels to a screen image. When images are blown up to fit into a large screen, therefore, it may be possible to see the individual dots. We recommend avoiding scaling images up above about 130 percent of the original size, unless you're going for an Atari or Commodore 64 effect.

## How Do I Show the Completed Images?

Images that have been digitized or created in the computer must be saved to a standard picture format and then placed into a presentation application for display. Some standard formats include JPEG, TIFF, BMP, and PICT. Most presentation programs will accept these and other formats. For an overview of available presentation software programs, refer to the Bonus Materials.

## How Much RAM and Hard Drive Space Do I Need?

Video chews up hard drive space. A typical two- or three-minute video production might take up 4GB of hard drive. The breakdown works like this: uncompressed video is 600k per frame, or 18MB per second. Video compressed at a 2:1 ratio, then, is 9MB per second, and 4:1 video is 4.5MB per second. Most computer systems are capable of playing video at 4:1 compression; data at this rate, then, takes up 270 MB per minute, not including audio. As you can see, it adds up quickly, which means that video processing on a computer used for making media shouldn't also share space with the church management software program.

Graphics are much easier to handle: a typical worship service of fifteen to twenty graphics can easily take up 50 MB, which multiplied by fifty-two times in a year equals 2.6 GB. Removable storage and recordable CD-ROMs make good archiving mediums for storing data from crowded computer desktops. Consider using two duplicate hard drives for archiving each year of your church's productions.

This means that to facilitate all this data around your computer, you're going to need lots of memory. RAM is relatively cheap and easy to get—and it is worth it the first time you have a crash in the middle of a worship service or presentation.

# AUDIO

## How Do I Handle Sound for My Video Clips?

Sound for movie and video clips should be routed through the facility sound system, particularly if the system is stereo. Most video decks have unbalanced audio outputs, which may be run directly to the soundboard.

If video is sent through a video switcher, and that switcher has audio capability, then all audio-for-video signals should be routed through the switcher, and the switcher output routed to the soundboard. Then audio levels may be monitored from the video board, with a static level established on the soundboard.

## What About All the Different Kinds of Microphones?

There are two basic types of microphones: **condenser** and **dynamic**.

Condenser microphones take many forms, including wireless lavalieres, gooseneck microphones located behind some podiums, suspended microphones hanging from the ceiling for choirs and singing groups, and clipped microphones used to amplify instruments. Condensers require a power source, which may be corded or battery-operated. Whereas instrumentalists prefer condenser microphones, dynamics are the favorite microphone of vocalists and speakers. Dynamic microphones respond better to the inflections of the human voice (hence the word: dynamic) and reproduce low frequencies well. They are reliable, withstand a certain degree of punishment, and may not require a separate power source.

Microphones come in two basic coverage types, as well. Some microphones are **omnidirectional**, meaning they pick up noise patterns in a 360° circumference. **Unidirectional** microphones, on the other hand, are limited to a certain degree to angle of what occurs around the top, or diaphragm, of the microphone. Among unidirectional microphones, **cardioid**, **supercardioid,** and **hypercardioid** all have certain advantages. The three have an increasingly narrower band of available space to pick up sound patterns. The ideal range for each of these microphones, defined as their "pickup angle," is defined in the following chart. Outside of the pickup angle, the output of the microphone is considerably lower.

| Omnidirectional | 360° |
|---|---|
| Cardioid | 131° |
| Supercardioid | 115° |
| Hypercardioid | 105° |

For more on audio amplification and reinforcement, purchase the *Yamaha Sound Reinforcement Handbook, Second Edition,* by Gary Davis and Ralph Jones (Hal Leonard Publishing; www.halleonard.com).

# PRESENTATION

## There Are Only 40,000 Projectors to Choose From . . .

The best way to understand the world of projectors is to break it down into feasible components. The first rating determines the brightness of a projector, or the ability it has to withstand ambient light. It is called the **ANSI lumens** rating. ANSI lumens are the most popular technical specification for determining projector quality. The higher the ANSI lumens number, the better the projector. Another important rating is the contrast ratio, or the difference that the projector makes between white and black. Again, higher is better.

Most affordable projection systems come in two popular digital flavors, LCD and DLP. Both are a single-lens style. DLP, pioneered by Texas Instruments, is the newer of the two technologies, although LCD is more ubiquitous and established. With either style, a minimum of 2,000 ANSI lumens is encouraged so that you can project an image without plunging the congregation into total darkness. Two thousand lumens isn't an absolute figure, for there are other variables that defy general categorizations. For more information, consult industry trade magazines or websites for periodic product reviews, which occur once or twice a year. See the Bonus Materials for more information.

Having low-maintenance equipment is equally as important as having high-quality equipment. If a high-quality piece of digital gear requires an engineer to operate, and no engineers are around, then that high-quality piece won't stay that way for long. Ditto if the best quality requires regular, expensive visits from the dealer's service department. There is little purpose to owning the most expensive piece of equipment if it can never maintain its original state. Some projectors may fall under this category: improperly converged or configured, you may end up with little green people on screen in worship. Whether this means buying a plug-n-play projector or setting up permanent cameras, do whatever is necessary to avoid needing the services of an engineer every weekend.

The most important thing to remember about the quality of your projected image is the role of ambient light in a room. The best image in the world cannot withstand the direct assault of light. Why do you suppose movie theaters are dark? If possible, explore rear-projection. If not possible, then focused light directed to places on the front platform can remove direct light from screens and allow even mediocre projectors to look fairly decent.

The second most important thing to remember about the quality of your projected image is the use of a screen. To save money, some churches project onto a white wall. This is a bad idea. Most paints absorb light, whereas screens reflect light. The same projector makes a much nicer image on a screen than on a wall. Additionally, a screen provides a nice frame for the image, which your congregations are used to seeing. Shooting onto a wall gives a more amateurish feeling.

## How Big a Screen Do I Need, and What Kind?

There is actually a rule for determining the best screen size for a particular space. Formulated by SMPTE, or the Society of Motion Picture and Television Engineers, the rule is called the 2x6 rule: the screen width should equal the distance in feet to the first row of seats, divided by two, and equal the distance to the last row of seats divided by six. In case the two are not the same, go with the larger figure. Screen height is then adjusted proportionally, adhering to either a 4:3 ratio or a 16:9 ratio. For example, as a very general estimate (don't just use this—measure your own!), a typical post–World War 2 church sanctuary (less than fifty years old) would need at least a twelve-foot-wide screen for a congregation of five hundred.

As mentioned, there is a difference between front- and rear-projection screens. Front screens are matte white, usually a reflective vinyl surface, whereas rear screens may be composed of vinyl, acrylic, or even glass that is nonreflective. Rear screens cost a bit more, but they are brighter and hide the projector. Since nearly all sanctuaries built in the pre-electronic era are designed to allow natural illumination, rear screens are preferable because they deal with ambient light better. On the other hand, unless you cover up the organ pipes or choir box, few sanctuaries have the extra room to allow for a rear-mounted projector. In this case, shutters or other options that convert light from natural to artificial might give you the ability to direct light away from the screen.

As far as number of screens, this depends on the physical space. Some rooms are so wide and shallow that multiple screens are crucial for proper viewing. But if possible, stick with one large screen. It keeps the congregation focused on the activity at hand, and in the line of sight for what is happening on stage, while avoiding the "tennis match" effect of having to look at either the live action or the image.

## How Can I Hook Together Several TVs?

Another low-cost option for small and beginning churches is to hook up several televisions to a single source such as a computer.

The best way to attach multiple monitors to a single source is through a **routing device**. The simplest router is an RF splitter, which splits a single RF signal into a number of signals. (You may have one of these on the floor of your living room, behind the television.) Although RF cable will maintain signal quality for up to one hundred or more feet, other kinds of video cable tend to lose signal quality. Hence the need for a device that can boost the signal as well as distribute it. Such devices are called **Distribution Amplifiers**, or DAs. It is wise to boost any split signal into multiple outputs.

Don't ever "Y" or "T" a signal without amplification, as the signal simply splits into two halves, which usually makes both too weak. Also, RF signal that will run across long stretches of cables (over one hundred feet) will need to be split through a DA because the signal begins to degrade.

# DUPLICATION

## Should We Record Worship Services for Distribution Audiocassette?

Duplication ministries serve a very useful ministry purpose, for both the community of believers at a local church and throughout the church universal. It is well documented that retention rates from oral presentations are pathetic in our digital culture. Beyond the addition of digital media as a part of the presentation, DVD, compact disc, and audiocassette copies provide a valuable tool for reinforcing core messages. They have a powerful dual impact when combined with memory or description of tangible, visual metaphors. Older congregants, who can no longer make it to weekly worship with regularity, also appreciate the opportunity to hear preaching and worship "virtually" with their congregation. Not only do they enrich, educate, and promote spiritual growth but audiocassettes can also be a handy evangelism tool for the workplace and to people in other geographic areas, which is of increasing importance in our aphysical, Internet world.

## OK, What Duplication Process Should I Use?

The most popular and efficient method is to duplicate through special duplicating machines. A number of companies sell audio duplicating machines that may be operated independently or hooked together. In the latter case the master is placed on one machine, and the others read from it as "slaves."

For more information, consult duplication specialists such as Kingdom Inc. at P.O. Box 506, Mansfield, PA 16933, 8007881122 (www.kingdom.com).

# OTHER IMPORTANT STUFF

## Where Can I Find Out More about the World of Digital Media?

There are a number of trade publications available free to media professionals (read: money-spenders) in order to keep up with the changing technology. Trades are helpful for becoming acclimated to the world of digital media, staying up on emerging technology, and finding companies offering media products and services. I first began learning about digital media through the world of trade magazines. Some include:

- *Church Production Magazine*, http://www.churchproduction.com/. Free trade publication targeting the church market. Lots of product reviews and producer/sanctuary profiles.
- *Digital Content Producer*, www.digitalcontentproducer.com. Free trade publication. Targets the professional industry, so the techno-talk can be daunting at first. Good product reviews and lots of industry contact information.
- *Digital Video* magazine, www.dv.com. Subscription fee, or free for professional subscriptions (you fill out a form on your church or company's media budget). A number of helpful product reviews and user tips in every issue.
- *Technologies for Worship Magazine*, http://www.tfwm.com/. Free trade publication targeting the church market. Lots of product reviews and producer/sanctuary profiles.

In addition, a number of user-focused websites provide real-world feedback on new products, creative productions, experiences, and situations. Some to check out include:

- Creative Cow, http://forums.creativecow.net/. The most popular user forum for production.
- Digital Media Net, http://www.digitalmedianet.com/. Lots of information, including a user forum.

CHAPTER 19

# THE PHASING PLAN

## WHY BUY TECHNOLOGY IN PHASES?

You may find that the best way to implement media technology into church life is through a series of purchasing phases over a planned length of time—for example, one phase per six months or year. Why phases? As opposed to one large purchase, phases may be appropriate to your situation for a number of reasons:

### Cost Involved

Most churches that begin media ministry don't have the luxury of incorporating it into a new facility but rather must integrate it into an existing environment that is not user-friendly. The unfriendly space often precludes a capital budget, which forces leaders to cast a vision for every penny. An initial phase or two may not only be cost-effective but may also lead to easier vision-casting, which in turn will lead to more funds for additional phases.

### Acceptance over Time

The second most stated comment from visitors experiencing media in worship for the first time, after expressing awe at the experience, is that it is a major production. Any foreign structure is always obvious on initial contact (including organs and stained glass), and the same is true for worship production. Although every form of worship is a form of production, from High Mass to campfire singing, most worshipers are oblivious to the form because it has become an intimate part of their experience. The best way to adapt a congregation to a new form is to introduce it in small enough increments that it is easily accepted.

A church in Oregon did this in such a way that the drive for media in worship became a process of responding to the congregation. The worship leader would show a movie clip one week, wait a few weeks for the furor to die down, show another, wait a few more weeks, and so on. Eventually the leader began to hear requests for more film clips and media use. Instead of fighting a theological battle with the congregation over worship forms, this worship leader planted seeds and then quenched the thirsty sprouts. Instead of the difficult battle of a "top-down" mandate, the media ministry became a grassroots church movement.

## Evolving Ideas for Use

Refer to part 1 on literacy. Once a church has been producing media for a while, it will begin to understand what sort of stories and messages can communicate best.

Capitalizing on these styles may dictate additional purchases. It is best initially not to purchase tools without knowing their potential use, lest they end up collecting dust. Again, ideas drive technology.

# PHASE 1: DISPLAY

## What You Get

The average local church worship attendance in America is just under ninety people,[1] which means a screen and projector is appropriate for all but the smallest of congregations. Luckily, projectors aren't nearly as expensive as when I first started on staff at Ginghamsburg. The projector I was hired to get in focus? It was 4,200 ANSI Lumens (the primary brightness rating for a video projector), as big as a Mini Cooper, and a steal of a secondhand deal at $80,000. Now they're roughly 1/100th as expensive.

## What You Need

There are basically two options:

- A video projector with a minimum of 2,000 ANSI lumens with a variety of computer and video ins and outs (I/O)
- Large projection screen
- A cart to put it on, a power strip and extension cord, and a set of cables to run between your sources and the projector

One option, the most commonly assumed, is to purchase a centrally located projector with a screen large enough to satisfy everyone, even the back row. Usually, in the context of the mid-twentieth-century rectangular worship spaces, this means a very large projector. As stated, be aware that the quality of a projector, unlike televisions, is dependent on the amount of ambient light surrounding it.

A severely cash-strapped congregation might instead consider:

- Four more TVs (27"+ screens)
- RF cables. Make them at least 25' long, or long enough to reach from one TV to another
- Stands or carts for each television
- Coaxial splitter (available at most electronics stores, for splitting the RF signal into four signals to route to the televisions)

Instead of one large screen, the second possibility is to set up multiple small screens throughout the worship space. An established rule of thumb is that a 27" television properly placed will service the viewing needs of up to fifty people. I would say maybe a 32" would serve fifty people a little better. These might be positioned as one in front on each side of the front of the worship space and one each along the side aisles halfway back.

Another option, for midsized or large congregations with long worship spaces, is to configure a combination of both options, with a projector in front and TVs in the rear.

## What It Costs

- Approximately $1,000 for TVs or $1,500-$2,000 for projector, not including screen and mounting costs

Entry-level projection systems run as low as $1,500, but one that fits the needs of most sanctuaries will cost a little more.

## Four Easy Steps to Purchasing a Projection System

Don't let the rapidly changing nature of digital media deter you from making a purchase. The shelf life of a unit is long enough to justify its expense. Remember that although nothing is really state of the art, it takes a very long time for a unit to become truly obsolete.

1. Find at least two trade magazine articles on projection systems.
2. Notice the few primary differences between the units, and mark these categories, with notes on each unit (see above on projector specifications).
3. Determine which categories speak best to your needs. For example, do you just need a video projector, or one with data input as well?
4. If available, have three local vendors bring units to your facility and show you what they look like in action. Try to convince the vendor to lend you a unit for a weekend service to view it in its context. Make sure to have some content to project! The most basic content for projection is a simple PowerPoint slideshow with announcements, song lyrics, and scripture. Once you are comfortable with your new projection system, you may be ready for Phase 2.

# PHASE 2: SHOWING PREPRODUCED VIDEO

## What You Get

Preproduced video allows you the ability to show high-quality films to illustrate and interpret messages in a visual context. Films can do what other media forms cannot. Early in my ministry, I showed a clip from the classic football film *Rudy* in a worship service on the theme of perseverance. *Rudy* is the tale of an undersized young man who through sheer will earns his place on a Notre Dame football team. The clip brought grown men to weeping. Manipulative? Maybe. I call it speaking in a language that people understand. (It's not any more manipulative than making people laugh with well-timed humor; the stigma is associated with crying.) The hook wasn't the clip itself; it was how we used the clip in the course of proclaiming the gospel.

Digital media, particularly video, is an inherently persuasive language tool. Video and graphics persuade through an appeal to senses, through an interpretation of the image, rather than through linear, analytical reasoning skills. This communication moves past head knowledge to the place where people's hearts become, as John Wesley once said so eloquently, "strangely warmed." Messages that speak in these ways are messages remembered long after their delivery. I don't remember much about the words or sentence structure of that sermon, but the *Rudy* clip inspires me to recall spiritual truth contained in that sermon: to persevere. As a dynamic contemporary metaphor that connects with a sport many people enjoy, it updates the athletic imagery that the Apostle Paul used for running a race or putting on the full armor of faith. A properly selected film clip, used with discretion (and without violating copyright), can accomplish the same thing for your message.

For more about the difference between the use of emotion and emotionalism, read the section on story in chapter 3 of *Digital Storytellers*.[2]

## What You Need

- A projection system, or—if you have not yet made that investment—an existing TV and video device such as a DVD/VCR, Apple TV, or current technology
- A film license
- A nearby video store or rental agreement with an online video service

## What It Costs

- $200-$500 for the film license, depending on average worship attendance, available from CVLI (http://www.cvli.com/). Refer to the online Bonus Materials for a more complete look at the copyright question.

# PHASE 3: COMPUTER TECHNOLOGY

## What You Get

Computers open up a world of graphic possibility and are the major step in realizing a church's potential to make media ministry integral to church life. Potential uses are discussed extensively in chapter 10. Beyond individual creative choices, however, with a computer the foundation has been set for the creation of original visual images, which is the key to interpretive digital media. Although the initial cost outlay is greater, computers are self-contained units, not needing weekly production expenditures, as with the older technologies. In addition, a computer is uniquely able to accommodate the last-minute whims of worship leaders.

## What You Need

- Any standard PC- or Macintosh-compatible computer system that you'd buy new at a computer store. The processing power of new systems is no longer a prohibitive factor in determining whether something is creatively possible.
- A 17" monitor or larger. Bigger monitors are crucial for graphic design.
- As much memory and hard drive storage space as you can handle.
- Some presentation software. Although the ubiquitous Microsoft Power-Point remains popular, a number of programs specifically geared toward the church market are now available. See the Bonus Materials for a review of many of the best options.
- A video/accelerator card for dual monitor display

There are many ways in which a computer can interface with a video device and TVs or projection. Outlined are four possibilities, on a scale of least expensive/quality to most expensive/quality, excepting the fourth option, which is high quality at a low rate, with one major caveat.

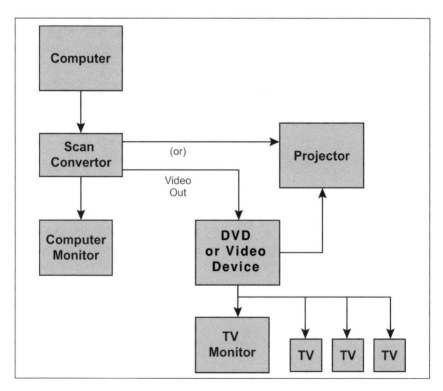

Option 1: Scan Converter

The monitor output of the computer plugs into the scan converter, and the scan converter plugs into the line input of a video device combo via video cable. The video device line output is then sent to the projection or monitor display. Scan converters work with a one-monitor system, or one "desktop." While presenting, there is no way to check the order of graphics on a separate computer display.

Some signal from the computer is lost in the transfer, but it is an inexpensive and easy way to mix computer graphics and video clips (somewhat) seamlessly into a presentation while avoiding the dreaded "Line 1" blue screen during the middle of worship. (Transitions during a service are crucial moments.)

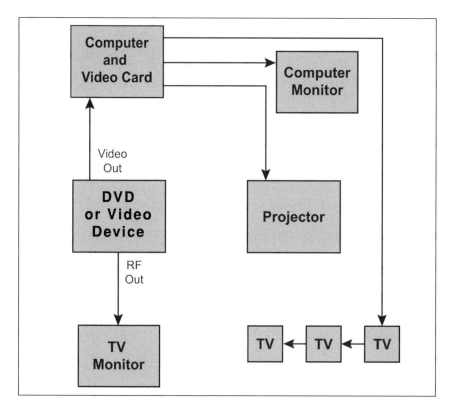

Option 2: Video Card, Post-video Device

Videos run from the video device into the computer through the video card line input, allowing an RGB (computer) signal to plug directly into a projector. This increases signal quality while eliminating the need for multiple inputs on a projector, and the subsequent dreaded mode shifting during worship. It also houses two monitor displays, giving the user the option to see individual graphics while in presentation mode.

Option 2 is slightly more expensive but the best option barring further expansion.

Another variation to this option is to eliminate the video player altogether and play clips directly through the computer via internal DVD drive. Many of the worship presentation programs outlined above have a feature that allows the user to play video clips off of DVD in the course of a presentation. This may be a better solution for small, "on-the-fly" operations that are operated by a single person.

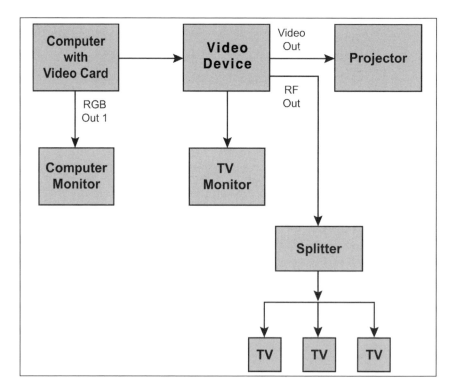

Option 3: Video Card, Pre-video Device

The computer output is sent via video cable into the line input of the video device, then to display. This one resembles Option 1, except it replaces an external scan conversion card with an internal video card, creating two monitor displays. It's better quality, but slightly more expensive. The best option for further expansion to video mixing is with live cameras. Many professionally installed systems will opt for this option.

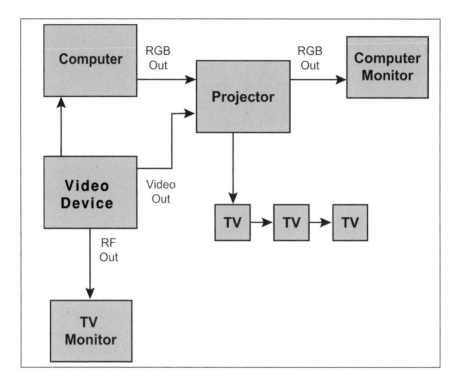

Option 4: Neither

Most projectors have separate RGB (computer) and video inputs, eliminating the need for conversion to video. Like option 1, this is a one-monitor configuration. This option will create the best inherent computer signal, but it forces the user to toggle between computer and video mode in worship. Least expensive, this option is best for computer display only, but worst for mixing video and computers, and only allows for the use of televisions via output from the projection.

## What It Costs

• $2,000-$3,000 for a computer system

A good computer system, outfitted as above, may cost approximately $1,500, not including some standard software. Presentation software runs from free to $450 or more. Scanners are $50 and up, but avoid the cheap ones, for the quality really begins to suffer. Secondary display video cards are $100 and up, and must include both an RGB out, which is advertised as an accelerator, and video ins and outs.

# PHASE 4: ORIGINAL GRAPHICS

## What You Get

You get the means to design and produce the graphic images detailed in part 2 and in the Bonus Materials. Creatively designed graphics separate effective media from boring business-style presentations composed of boring solid-color gradients and opaque, fully offset drop shadows. The objective is not to create computer effects. Strive for a television look rather than a computer look.

Original graphics bring a higher potential for interpretation. Instead of repeating the text of a scripture reading on screen during a sermon, an illustration—either original or derived from stock photography—can persuade using postliterate language. Good models for effective graphics can come from cable television, the Internet, and more. Sports channels such as ESPN, or programming and station identification on networks like the History Channel, Arts and Entertainment, and CNN epitomize television graphics—bold, colorful, with depth. Strive for these styles, and along the way introduce photography—stock and your own—with frames, edges, and montages. See the design section in part 2 for more details.

## What You Need

- Image manipulation software. Adobe Photoshop is the standard, but other tools work fine. While Photoshop is expensive (more than $600 at full retail), church discounts are available. Also consider Photoshop Elements, a low-cost consumer alternative with many features, or even GIMPshop, a free open-source image manipulation program (http://gimpshopdotnet.blogspot.com/). Photoshop plug-ins, or add-in features, aren't necessary but are very helpful for those occasions when pressed for time. Mostly plug-ins allow the user to create specific treatment easily. (Actually they're quite dangerous from a design perspective. Make sure you only use plug-ins that correspond with design intentionality.)

- A digital camera and a thirty-bit color flatbed scanner for raw and original image capturing.
- Removable storage capability for transfer and archiving. Even handheld portable drives will work.

For nonartists, or beginning graphic artists, there are many ways to accelerate your learning curve. A variety of sources offer preproduced images and art for free or for a small fee. Refer to the Bonus Materials for more information and website addresses.

## What It Costs

- $1,600

There's no limit to the amount of money one can spend on software and source image material with all the extras that are on the market. Count on spending at least $600 to $800 to get started. Basic image acquisition hardware, whether scanner or camera, varies, though prices continue to fall on digital cameras. Scanners are best for flat images, like photographs, whereas digital cameras are best for any three-dimensional object, like a bottle, car, or building. Be careful with $49 scanners that may be junk.

# PHASE 5: ORIGINAL VIDEO

## What You Get

The power of the creative juice gushing from your teams will eventually overtake the technical hurdle of creating original video. Video opens up a world of potential to worship or teaching experience. For example, testimonies edited to two minutes, with background music and environment shots, can tell a story much more powerfully than a twenty-minute microphone exposition. Montages can create a mood to match a message in drama, music, or the spoken word. Brief visual narratives, of the sort found in contemporary commercials, can set up the metaphor for an event. With digital technology, there are fewer limits to the creative mind. As with Phase 4, see chapter 10 for more uses.

The jump from Phase 4 to 5 is large, as good-quality video has a steep learning curve. Fortunately for congregational amateurs, "reality TV" and YouTube have made homemade video acceptable.

# What You Need

## A Means of Acquiring Video with Audio
- Industrial-level three-chip DV format or direct-to-hard-drive camcorder
- Professional audio (XLR) input adapter, depending on the camera (some cameras have this feature built in)
- Clip-on and dynamic microphones with supporting XLR cables
- Camera-mounted lights or a field lighting kit
- Tripod for stable shooting

## A Means of Editing Video
- Macintosh- or PC-compatible professional model computer with dual monitors and mid-level to high-performance RAM and processing power. Although one can edit with an older system, if possible always buy state-of-the-art, as it lasts much longer and is worth the investment.
- As much storage space as you can afford
- 20" or larger video monitor for watching video output
- Video capture card (for retrieving digital video in and out)
- Nonlinear video editing software
- Stock music CDs

In the 1990s, computer technology overturned conventional wisdom on editing. As opposed to old paradigms of literally cutting film, or of linear, dual-deck video editing, computers allow a producer to edit in **nonlinear** form. The transition is analogous to the move from typewriters to word processors. A typeset word could only be changed with a bottle of 1x3 paper slip or whiteout, and its physical proximity on a page was permanent. Similarly, linear video editing is the ordered sequence of shots applied to videotape, and reordering of the sequence would require a completely new edit. Word processing has allowed users to figuratively cut and paste sections of a document, composing and ordering thoughts in a nonlinear fashion or method that matches the creative process of most persons. Nonlinear video is the visual equivalent, a process that frees the mind to concentrate on the narrative as opposed to its construction. These advances are making it possible for amateurs to create incredible video. It is the democratization of media. It is the cultural shift from text to image.

Early nonlinear digital video editing schemes (NLE, to industry insiders) were extremely expensive, costing buyers $50,000 and more to convert analog video to the digital realm and back again. While professional shops still use expensive software, now programs geared toward consumers, such as Apple's iMovie, Microsoft's Movie Maker, and Avid Free DV, are free. This means that a user only needs the right kind of computer, a video monitor, and software to create incredible video.

Another possible need during the postproduction process is stock music. Stock (or "buyout") music is composition created for the purpose of accompanying video. Arrangements can be made with clearinghouses to purchase CDs of stock music, which come with a copyright clearance for usage. Prices may range from $40 per CD to thousands of dollars for a library. (See part 2.) Also, software such as SonicPro and Apple's Garage Band can create custom musical scores.

Related to scoring music is sound effects, which can add a lot to a video. Individual sound effects for diverse subjects are available through many websites, such as sounddogs.com, for immediate download and use.

### A Means of Presenting the Video

Basically, there are two ways to present videos created in the digital realm: remain in the digital realm or "dump" to tape. In the digital realm, clips can be played directly from the editing software or converted to a self-contained, compressed video clip to be played through presentation software. "Dumping" is the process of mastering a video from the editing system to videotape for playback in a traditional videotape deck.

## What It Costs

For the whole job, it will cost at least anywhere from $5,000-$20,000 or more, depending on camera and postproduction systems.

- A video camera for image acquisition. A midrange, 3-chip DV format camera does a wonderful job and only requires a small adapter to receive professional audio input: $3,000.
- Audio for video, including a cardioid and a dynamic microphone and audio cables: $1,000 or more.
- A camera mounted light: $200.
- Bags and production storage: $300.
- An entry-level nonlinear video editing system, with software and third-party boards: free to $15,000 or more.
- Good quality audio monitors: $500 or more.
- Stock music and videotape: $500 or more.

# PHASE 6: CAMERAS

Though some naysayers object to the "studio" feel that may result if in-worship cameras are conspicuously placed, cameras can serve a very valuable function in worship. Many sanctuaries have a number of badly positioned seats, which might be defined as any seat more than fifty feet away from the platform, or any seat with an obstructed view. This is problematic because preaching, an oral form, relies heavily on the facial expressions and body movements of the preacher. Closer views are also necessary for dramas and skits, as well as liturgical elements such as baptism.

## What You Get

Live switching is the most expensive of all the phases, but the most necessary for large congregations. In a congregation of more than one thousand in worship, there cannot be one thousand good seats, but unlike managers of theaters and sports arenas, church leaders are gravely concerned that the people in the rear have an experience equally as good as that of people sitting in front. This means bringing the activities of the platform to where they are.

Good use of cameras in a live worship event achieves this task of creating intimacy. It can also capture events otherwise unseen, such as baptism close-ups. Further, the presence of live cameras can enhance the meaning of a live event. For example, the experience of a piece of music becomes more complete for the worshiper in the digital culture when confronted by a visual interpretation of the song, whether that is a narrative form or a re-creation of the performance for a visual context. Sermon retention rates rise with the addition of visual listening forms to accompany oral presentation.

## What You Need

There are actually two hardware considerations to this phase. The first is the addition of the video switcher or mixer. This device coordinates the various signals, provides a means to switch or toggle between them, and sends them out to a common output. Mixers also contain a variety of wipe and dissolve options, and many feature **keying** ability. Keying a color removes it from the video signal and overlays the signal onto another video signal.

Television meteorologists use one type of keying, chroma, to give the weather forecast over computerized maps (another type of keying, luminance or luma key, is popular in video postproduction). Most broadcast facilities use large switchers containing sixteen or more inputs; live events for the life of the church will suffice with approximately eight inputs, including computer, video (1-2), and cameras (3-5 or more, with extra inputs installed in unique locations for special events).

The second hardware consideration is the cameras themselves. Live cameras are the final, most professional stage of managing a media ministry, and they require the most from the teams of volunteers involved. Professional broadcast-quality studio cameras are necessary; industrial-level cameras will suffice, with proper installation and a good mixing console to integrate the variety of live, computerized, and video sources. Here is one possible configuration, based on a three-camera setup:

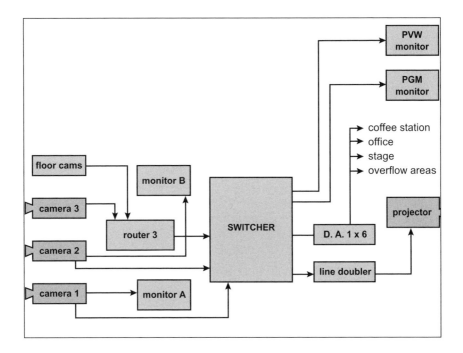

## What It Costs

- Two or three industrial-quality studio cameras: $7,000 each
- Support equipment for cameras (pedestals, camera controls): $2,500 each
- Video cabling: $1,000

- Video mixing console with conversion (for RGB) or synchronization (for video): $4,000
- Monitors for multiple sources: 5 at $400 each, totaling $2,000

## The Final Configuration

With everything combined, a final media schematic might look like this:

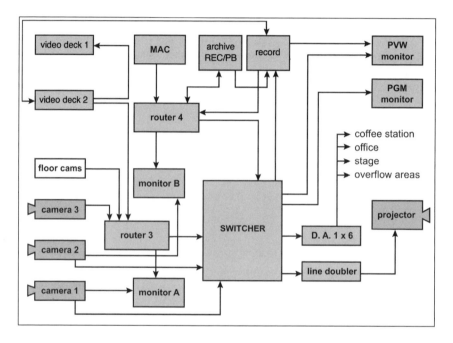

All the phases together add up to a big bill, but do not forget the purpose of phases, which allow a congregation to implement media over time as needed for worship. Further, do not forget the primary purpose for pursuing media ministry. Communication is not about budgets but about changing lives. One church in Pennsylvania, averaging 600 worshipers a weekend during two Sunday morning services, began what they termed a media-driven worship service based on a seven-team structure of hospitality, drama, computer graphics, video, audio/lighting, music, and resource/worship planning. The service was targeted to the unchurched of the local community. By its tenth week, the new service was up to 150 people, raising the church's weekend population by 25 percent. As one church administrator said, "Technology is just the cost of doing business in this culture."

# CONCLUSION

A church in Connecticut has reversed long-term decline through the use of media. The pastor told me, "Worship attendance is up 13 percent in the past year. Given our recent history, even a net change of zero would be a plus." Saying that the use of media has generated excitement equivalent to a new church start, the pastor has witnessed a dramatic increase in mission involvement and giving. Further, many new young families and faces have begun to pepper a traditionally aged crowd on Sunday mornings. He anticipates a second worship service to begin in the fall.

A young college graduate at a state school in Ohio began advertising for a campus media ministry start-up. The response was so great that he did not have adequate systems in place and had to turn away scores of eager people while he left campus to raise funding for equipment and facilities. Those young people were excited by the opportunity to use their creative and technological talents for the glory of God.

A small, rural congregation in Illinois played a video emphasizing the empty tomb on Easter morning, matched the sermon title to the video ("Beyond the Tomb"), used images to bring the theme together, and even replayed the same clip later without audio under a special song. The result was, as one woman related, "Awesome and relevant. It was powerful, and truly experiential."

A large, established church in a wealthy suburb spent over a million dollars on a renovated sanctuary with a new organ and many traditional accoutrements in 1996. By 2006, it was faced with the difficult decision of how to integrate digital technology into a space for which it was not designed when the contemporary service, meeting in the church gymnasium and using visual media, began to outpace the "main service." They realized their mistake, but celebrated the lives changed by what they had considered their "alternative" service.

A multicultural mainline congregation in New York City used innovative media to transcend boundaries through art and technology. The congregation has four primary language groups that come together to experience worship in a larger community of 150 language groups, but they learned to use visual projection to break down those barriers. The congregation creates what the pastor has called "wordless worship" by using imagery to make biblical connections.

A church plant meeting in a YMCA overcame the challenge of building community in a temporary space by telling stories through visual and interactive means. In the course of one service, people went from being strangers to crying and hugging as friends as they shared their own stories inspired by the story presented on screen.

These are stories of life transformation brought about by the use of media in ministry.

It would be a disservice to try to argue that pursuing the goal of worshiping with digital media, in a visual fashion, is easy. It presents very real challenges in terms of money, time commitments, laity support and commitment, vision-casting, and learning a complex new industry, to name a few. Being a disciple is not all about blue skies, as Jesus so eloquently reminds us in Luke 12:49-56. Fortunately for us we have the power of the Holy Spirit to guide us in this new digital wilderness. Ultimately, the reward is worth the pain and toil, as churches grow and lives are transformed into the likeness of Christ. This is the goal and desire of any ministry conducted in the name of Jesus Christ.

Visit
www.thewiredchurch2.com
for Bonus Materials
including:

- Sources for Preproduced Worship Media
- A Review of Worship Presentation Software
- How to Make an "On the Street" Video
- How to Make a Time-Lapse Video
- How to Make Better Song Lyrics Slides
- Media Ministry Job Functions
- Introduction to Media Copyright
- Pre-event Technical Checklist
- Director's Commands and Sample Script
- A Glossary of Media Terms

# NOTES

## 1. UNDERSTANDING DIGITAL MEDIA

1. What an ironic word: iconoclast, or "image breaker," referred originally to the forerunners who, 500 years ago, suggested the church become more effective communicators by embracing the new technology of mass print media and move away from the stale traditions of image, experience, and "smells and bells."

2. Mass print is one of many macrosystems that have categorized the communication styles of civilization throughout history. Communication typologies, or means of categorizing these systems, have been well documented.

## 2. FOUR WAYS TO UNDERSTAND MEDIA IN MINISTRY

1. "Right Before Our Eyes," Christopher Porterfield, *Time* magazine, June 6, 1998, 69.

2. This statement, written in 1998 for *The Wired Church*, is already proving prophetic with the rise of YouTube, where everyone is a producer (their tagline is "Broadcast Yourself") and MySpace and Facebook, where everyone is a web designer. The next step in this graphicacy is design.

## 3. THE SHAPE OF THIS CULTURAL LANGUAGE

1. "Epilogue: Advancing on the Path of Righteousness (Maybe)," George Gerbner, *Cultivation Analysis: New Directions in Media Effects Research*, N. Signorielli and M. Morgan, eds. (unpublished), 250.

2. To understand what this means and examine some other categories for understanding the Christian role in the culture, read *Christ and Culture* (1949), by H. Richard Neibuhr, which has been getting recent respect again. Then read *Resident Aliens* by Stanley Hauerwas and William Willimon (Nashville: Abingdon Press, 1989), for a counter view. These are required reading for anyone trying to integrate cultural language into church life.

3. Mitchell Stephens, *The Rise of the Image, the Fall of the Word* (New York: Oxford, 1998), 23.

4. Ibid., 30.

5. Ibid., 91.

6. Tom Boomershine, "The Polish Cavalry and Christianity in Electronic Culture," *United Seminary Journal of Theology*, 1996, 4.

7. "God's Little Toys," William Gibson, *Wired* magazine, July 2005, http://www.wired.com/wired/archive/13.07/gibson.html.

8. Neil Postman, *Amusing Ourselves to Death: Public Discourse in the Age of Show Business* (New York: Penguin Books, 1985), 118.

9. Steven Spielberg, *Mr. Showbiz* interview, June 28, 1998, www.mrshowbiz.com.

## 4. THE "ENTERTAINMENT" QUESTION

1. A common assertion from critical books such as Neil Postman's *Amusing Ourselves to Death* and Gregor Goethals' *The Electronic Golden Calf: Images, Religion and the Making of Money*, which are both products of highly literate practitioners who may sense obsolescence.

2. It may be the last generation, though, as the passive medium of television gives way to the cultural forums and channels of the Internet. At the very least, what we presently think of as television will shift as Internet technology converges.

3. Stephens, 29-30.

4. Walter Bagehot, *Physics and Politics* (New York: Cosimo Classics, 2007), 105.

## 5. CONCURRENTLY CULTURAL AND COUNTERCULTURAL

1. http://www.ntslibrary.com/Online-Library-How-Could-Jesus-Be-Both-Divine-and-Human.htm.

2. Dave Wehrle, posted online at http://midnightoilproductions.com/reading/?p=26, March 28, 2006.

## 7. VISUAL PREACHING AND WORSHIP PLANNING

1. Fred B. Craddock, *As One without Authority: Fourth Edition Revised and with New Sermons* (St. Louis: Chalice Press, 2001), 18.

2. Andy Stanley and Ronald L. Jones, *Communicating for a Change* (Colorado Springs: Multnomah Books, 2006), 103.

## 8. BASICS FOR BUILDING VISUAL ELEMENTS

1. http://www.christianitytoday.com/history/special/131christians/clement.html

2. Jason Moore and Len Wilson, *Design Matters: Creating Powerful Imagery for Worship* (Nashville: Abingdon Press, 2006), 28.

## 11. ESTABLISH THE GAME PLAN

1. Wayne Cordeiro, *Doing Church as a Team* (New Hope Publishing: Honolulu, 1998), 120.

2. Ibid., 154.

## 16. A STORY ON GETTING STARTED

1. By referencing Midnight Oil, Bill is referring to the equipping part of our ministry. Bill hosted our one-day teaching seminar. The seminar, which emphasizes using digital media to connect people to the gospel story in ways that make sense for our present digital culture, affirmed for Bill many of the things he was already doing. See http://www.midnightoilproductions.com/seminar to learn more.

## 17. LESSONS ON THE USE OF TECHNOLOGY

1. Why, then, you say, do Hollywood studios continue to spend so much? Because artists' dreams always outpace technology, and advances in technology encourage riskier creations. It's the same reason that futuristic visions of automatic kitchens turned into the reality of increased time spent cooking and cleaning. The law of accelerated culture is at work.

## 19. THE PHASING PLAN

1. The Barna Update: "Small Churches Struggle to Grow Because of the People They Attract" (The Barna Group, September 3, 2003), www.barna.org.

2. Len Wilson and Jason Moore, *Digital Storytellers: The Art of Communicating the Gospel* (Nashville: Abingdon Press, 2002).